ADAM'S

DREAM

ADAM'S DREAM

DREAM

A Preface to
Translation

by

Ben Belitt

GROVE PRESS, INC., NEW YORK

First Edition 1978
First Printing 1978
ISBN: 0-394-50288-4
Grove Press ISBN: 0-8021-0166-6
Library of Congress Catalog Card Number: 78-51399

First Evergreen Edition 1978
First Printing 1978
ISBN: 0-394-17066-0
Grove Press ISBN: 0-8021-4217-6
Library of Congress Catalog Card Number: 78-51399

Library of Congress Cataloging in Publication Data

Belitt, Ben, 1911-
  Adam's dream.

  Bibliography: p.
  1. Poetry—Translating—Addresses, essays, lectures.
  2. Neruda, Pablo, 1904-1973—Addresses, essays, lectures.
  I. Title.
  PN1059.T7B4 1978   418'.02   78-51399
  ISBN 0-394-50288-4
  ISBN 0-394-17066-0 pbk.

Edited and designed by Susan Harper at the Scrimshaw Press

Jacket design: Cristina Simoni

Manufactured in the United States of America

Distributed by Random House, Inc., New York

GROVE PRESS, INC., 196 West Houston Street, New York, N.Y. 10014

"*The Imagination may be compared
to Adam's dream—he awoke
and found it truth.*"

—John Keats to Bailey
November 22, 1817

For Bernard Malamud

" 'First do a decent drawing . . .'
" 'What about the truth of colors?"
—Idiots First: "Naked Nude"

CONTENTS

PREFACE

I am aware that the claim to be made for this book of prefaces must be a modest one. In a sense, the collection has been thrust upon me by the occupational irony of things which has ordained that prefaces to translations will generally go unread, or be regarded as exercises in gratuitous self-incrimination. The reader, in his haste to get on with the text, has little interest in the history of the ordeals which produced it; and nothing will mollify the misgivings of those whose expectations remain ungratified. It has seemed helpful to me, therefore, to disengage the prefatory rites of extenuation from the occasions which produced them over a thirty-year interval of apprenticeship. They were "prefaces" *once* because they literally preceded the English of a bilingual transaction, and because what remained primary was the French or the Spanish of their complex and exacting originals. Their function *then* was to confide or exhort or placate; their function *now* is to furnish a simultaneous record of "theory and practice" that is ontological rather than propitiatory in character.

For what it is worth, then, this is a "casebook" on translation, *after the fact*, with all the contradictions and restatements innate to a function in search of its criteria. The sections on theory and practice should be read as an on-going improvisation, a rough estimate of the translator's accountability for his procedures after, and not in advance of, his word-for-word encounter with the originals. The assumption that theory should precede practice is as erroneous as the assumption that a poetics of tragedy must precede the *Oresteia* of Aeschylus, or a cosmology, the word of God. Translation is nothing if not empirical, wayward, doubt-ridden, immediate. The translator, *in medias res*, addresses himself not to the history of polemics, but to the particulars of a transaction whose completion as a linguistic artifact must remain inductive. Only afterward does it serve as a "case in point" or a datum in a "theory of translation."

In my own case, theory has come as a consequence of my reflection on the artifacts of others, or the controversy into which all translators are drawn in their pursuit of an equivocal undertaking. I do not feel any the wiser after three decades of practice and contemplation, or any readier for a terminal poetics of translation which will assure me of the truths dreamt by Adam and lost to the rest of us, as George Steiner has suggested, "after Babel." Where my posture is defensive, it has been in the interests of latitude, rather than certitude. What I think must be confronted as curiously as Professor Steiner has confronted it, is the plurality of the options which are generally conceded to the poet, but denied his translator. I am certain only of the rightness of the posture which has constantly forced me back to the point at which poetry itself is thought to begin: Imagination. As a translator, I do not know how to un-think imagination in the translation of poetry; and in thinking about poetry, I do not know how to revoke the enfranchising heresy of Coleridge that "the immediate aim of poetry is pleasure, and not truth." All translation is in process of retranslation, in a way that the initiating texts, wholly at home in their imaginative autonomy, are not. A casebook such as this can only testify to the search for living utterance in the realm of imagined equivalences.

The final section on the "oeuvre" of Pablo Neruda is by no means peripheral to a "casebook on translation." The case that it presents is the hermeneutical one of construing the original as a context innate to itself, rather than a textual equation in progress. As such, it constitutes a further dimension of translation. All critics "translate" (as Professor Steiner has ably demonstrated), and all translators are presented with command decisions along the way involving the fastidious exercise of critical choices. Both may be regarded as modes of *reading*, as well as writing; and no one is likely to read a foreign text as obsessively as a translator, for whom every word is a confrontation and every choice, a visible commitment. The provisional character of my approach to a context for Neruda's oeuvre in the concluding essays will be apparent from their constant "revaluation" of the available evidence, the literal weighting and piecing together of the parts as they emerge from the enlargement of the poet's canon and the tempering of his vision. I have tried to suggest both the diversity of that vision and its importance for the literature of one world and a single community of tradition, rather than a symptomatic "third" of it. In this sense, too, I have "translated" in the spirit of Adam's dream, for the "truths of the imagination."

My thanks are due the following publications and publishers for permission to reprint the essays included in this volume: *Review* 74 for "The Translator as Nobody in Particular," *Salmagundi* for "*Imitations*:

Translation as Personal Mode," Farrar, Straus & Giroux for "Neruda's *Joaquín Murieta*: A Note on the Poetics of Translation," Edwin Honig and *Modern Poetry Studies* for "Translation as Adam's Dream: A Conversation with Edwin Honig," Swallow Press for "Towards a Translation of Rimbaud," Grove Press for the prefaces to *Poet in New York*, *Selected Poems of Pablo Neruda*, "The Moving Finger and the Unknown Neruda," and "Pablo Neruda: A Revaluation," the University of California Press for the prefaces to *Juan de Mairena* and the *Selected Poems of Rafael Alberti*, *The Bennington Review* for "Neruda's *Memoirs*: A Reading from Homer," and *Modern Poetry Studies* for "Pablo Neruda: Splendor and Death."

Two of the sections in "Pablo Neruda: A Revaluation" have also appeared in Spanish translations: "The Mourning Neruda" as "Neruda Enlutado" in *Mundo Nuevo* (Paris) and "The Burning Sarcophagus" as "El Sarcófago en Llamas" in *Razón y Fábula* (Bogotá). Segments of the same essay have also appeared in *Southern Review*, *Voyages*, and *Mundus Artium*.

I am indebted to Susan Harper, Jo Carson Rider, and Frederick Mitchell of The Scrimshaw Press for helpful suggestions which have given this volume of essays its present contour. I am also happy to acknowledge the interest and support of the Center for Inter-American Relations.

Ben Belitt
Bennington College, Vermont
April 1978

I

Translation as Adam's Dream:

A Conversation

*One translates as Forster's
Professor Godbole prays, singing
one's odd little tune and saying
"Come! Come! Come! Come!"*

Translation as Adam's Dream:
A Conversation

Time: *Saturday, October 4, 1975*
Place: *"The Old Firehouse," North Bennington, Vermont*
Participants: *Edwin Honig and Ben Belitt*

Edwin Honig   I'd like to begin by asking how you started translating, since the experience of each translator is rather different. In the case of some poets like John Hollander, translation came as a kind of apprenticeship to the writing of poetry. That is, for John, as he described it, doing translations was the "grammar" for his poetic development. Of course, many poets don't translate at all, or don't know language well enough to do it. But what was it like in your case?

Ben Belitt   I would agree that translation is a kind of jungle gym for the exercise of all the faculties and muscles required for the practice of poetry, even if it doesn't always begin that way—that it serves the calesthenic function of bringing to bear upon what is translated one's total resources and cunning as a poet. In this sense, translation takes the translator far beyond the genre of his own recognizable style and idiosyncrasies as a poet. One of the disintegrative benefits of translation is that it compels or seduces one into writing poetry other than one's own, and exercises faculties alien to one's genre as a practicing poet.

E. H.   When were you aware that you were translating in a literary way for the first time?

B. B.   I suppose it first came as a by-product of my close reading of the French Symbolist poets with Wallace Fowlie at Bennington, as a kind of unofficial seminar exclusively invented for my benefit between 1937-1940. It was the idiom of Rimbaud, I remember, which excited and gratified me most at the time. My knowledge of French was such that, although I could imagine what the tension and weight of the idiom was in French, I couldn't get close enough to the sound and excitement of it without *touching it with English* and, as Keats says, "proving it on my own pulses."

E. H.   A good phrase . . . "on my own pulses." So you started with Rimbaud as a poet whose language and style were very sympathetic.

B. B.   More than sympathetic. I felt an invisible opening for myself somewhere under the French, as a poet in search of a language that *mattered*. I was looking for accelerations, truncations, oddity, energy, character—everything one associates with the high tensions and syntactical speeds of Rimbaud.

E. H.   Do you remember any poems in particular?

B. B.   Any number of them: especially, the four chosen for inclusion in the volume itself—*Le Bateau Ivre, Les Premiers Communions, Mémoires, Les Poétes de Sept Ans*. All turned into "personal versions" the moment I touched them with a little English, as a kind of venture in private acoustics. I wanted to "score" Rimbaud in a way that was identical with my own *hearing*, rather than constantly making allowances for correspondences I was told should exist for all sensitive Frenchmen: I longed for the immediacy of poetry in English while still parsing the French and computing alexandrines. I set about "translating" Rimbaud as a greedy amateur for my own instruction and pleasure because I was imprudently (or helplessly) drawn to the four ambitious set-pieces I published as *Four Poems by Rimbaud: The Problem of Translation*. The title was a later deception of an English publisher, which promised more than it delivered, since I didn't treat the "problem" discursively at all. There was only a very brief preface which rebelled at "turning francs into dollars," and said the first things beginners ought to say. The scheme of that volume was two-fold: to make a set of avowedly literal translations as grubby as fidelity seemed to demand—transliterate French staples into English; and then to put a pulse under the English and "translate the translations" in the sense that I tried to project qualities, identities, skills, predilections, textures—my own, such as they were, and Rimbaud's, such as I imagined them to be.

E. H.   What Dryden called "paraphrase" rather than literal translation or imitation . . .

B. B.   I don't know whether either of those words really applies. It was something more subjective than imitation and more visceral than paraphrase. I had no conceptual stance which would lead me to say: "Here I'm going to paraphrase"; or "Here is where I imitate." Paraphrase was *there* when required or stumbled on; but so were fidelity, imitation, and what Stevens called "the pleasures of merely circulating."

E. H.   The scheme of the book, as you say, called for the literal rendering first and the "personal version" after.

B. B.   Only to indicate how inadequate poetry in its literal state can be —to make the point that poetry was not *information*, that the translator's task had only begun when all the facts of syntax and substance had been reliably extrapolated. The point was to isolate *something else*—something absent or missing—by maximizing the vacuum where all had been suspended in the search for meanings and was now in danger of disappearing entirely from the transaction: *the power of imagination.* How do you imagine or re-imagine the process of a poem's embodiment—the poem not as an informative entity, but as a complex—I believe Coleridge called it esemplastic—of immediate excitements that stand for a live experience?

E. H.   But evidently, if this work, as you describe it, was your first, you already had a kind of theoretical or didactic interest in the subject—or the "problem"—of translation.

B. B.   No, I would say I stumbled on translation in the process of trying to find something which was cognate with my experience of having thought about a poet, read him word-for-word and word-by-word, and then found it hostile or insipid to paraphrase. Let us say I invoked a "pleasure principle" rather than a homiletic one, that my approach was hedonistic rather than Aristotelean, much as Coleridge does when he says the "immediate aim of poetry is pleasure and not truth." I would be quite as ready to say that the *immediate* aim of translation is pleasure and not truth. Eventually, of course, immediate pleasure leads to imaginable truth. The two are not necessarily antithetical.

E. H.   Well, there you have a principle! It's very hard to get working translators to say what they really think translation is for, or about. In the case of poets, it's almost always that, isn't it?

B. B.   Always what?

E. H.   Always an attempt to render the pleasure, the experience of immediate pleasure, *knowingly*. Were you aware of any sort of transfusion going on from your translation into the poem?

B. B.   Translation is a way of working and living, or writing and breathing, and not a public benefaction. It would be altogether wishful to imagine I had turned into something Rimbaldian myself. But looking back at my development at the time, I would say that there was a conspicuous thrust—an infusion rather than a transformation of my purposes as a poet—which was all to the good. If may be there to this day—but that is for others skilled in "the anxieties of influence" to determine.

E. H.   Where do you fit your Rimbaud translations into your own oeuvre as a poet?

B. B.   In a limbo I vaguely remember as one of marked disjunctions and escalations of style that had something to do with my previous collision with Hart Crane in 1936. I sensed something then, which has now been abundantly researched and certified: that there had also been a collision of Rimbaud with Crane, and I was dizzy with the hovering ambiguity. I was already enroute to a kind of impasto, or density, of language—crisscrossed by all the short circuits and shifts of speed I coveted in both the French of Rimbaud and the latter-day Elizabethan of Crane. The last poem to go into my first collection, a poem called "The Enemy Joy" at some times, and " 'Tarry, Delight' " at others, was a direct outcome of my translation.

E. H.   Now, if I'm not mistaken, your reputation as a translator is based mainly on your translations from the Spanish, rather than the French or Italian.

B. B.   True. However, in my long apprenticeship to Wallace Fowlie I read Baudelaire for the first time, Mallarmé, Valéry, Corbiére, LaForgue, Apollinaire . . .

E. H.   All the significant "moderns."

B. B.   What we were really doing was *dowsing*. Wherever I felt a pull of the language or picked up a possibility that jolted my interests, I made a decided bend in that direction.

E. H.   There's another aspect that ought to concern us—this conjunction of three minds—two poets sharing a literary experience involving an exchange of literatures.

B. B.   In return for Rimbaud I read Fowlie some of Hart Crane, whom he found more difficult than Valéry.

E. H.   I had a conversation a few days ago with Herb Mason, who did a remarkable job of the Gilgamesh epic and whose languages are not modern or Romantic generally, but Arabic, Turkish. . . . Mason's experience was unusual. As he says, he doesn't want to call it translation. He came to the story of the Gilgamesh epic, which is about the loss of a friend, partly as a result of his own personal losses, and for several years after he kept sharing the poem with others—not just anybody, but with certain people he felt were sympathetic. After four years of this, he was ready to write what he calls his verse-narrative based on the Gilgamesh epic. He subsequently learned Akkadian. Now, the poem doesn't exist in terms of a text; there are only scrambled lines. That's another subject we ought to get into—the absent text—because I think it's not just in the ancient Homeric epic poems that one is forced to deal with the lack of an established text, but even in moderns like Lorca. I hadn't been aware, till speaking with Mason, of how such a conjunction induces a strong, if gradual, drive to tackle the work, especially in the early phases of one's interest in translation.

B. B.   I imagine it would differ in relation to the media in which the originals exist. Certainly, for poetry, I would say translation is neither a solitary vice nor a collective voice. It is an attempt to express one's own exuberance or one's own sense of contact with things. I myself don't know how to separate my own voice from the initiating voices because the initiating voices furnish a continuing motive for my own. There are two voices, two presences. That has never really changed. For me, translation remains the sensuous approximation of an amateur—a histrionic projection of my visceral and intellectual fascinations—and, I would always want to add, my *pleasure*. Translation should always give pleasure.

E. H.   You go along with Wallace Stevens there, on his tour of "supreme fictions."

B. B.   Particularly the translation of *poetry*. I'm totally Coleridgean in that sense, as I believe Stevens may have been, too. I do believe that there ought to be an "immediate" consequence to the translation of poetry itself. And the immediate consequence of poetry, the immediate embodiment of language as a sensuous texture of intentions and utterances, is pleasure—pleasure first, and then truth. Then, on and on, into the refinements of the initiating artifact.

E. H.   Speaking of "absent texts," the pleasure could also be that of sharing something with the absent author whom one is translating. You translated Neruda later, and a great deal.

B. B   Abundantly, because the man himself was abundant. Because no one else was doing it abundantly at the time. Because Neruda was pleased with the renderings and the choices, and abundantly encouraged me to translate.

E. H.   That's a case in which one knows one's source; I mean the "originating poet." (I don't know about these terms.)

B. B.   I believe you mean there is a difference between posthumous translations of Dante and Shakespeare, and translating an extant poet who may thereafter see all you have done over and under his name, certify it, or recoil in horror?

E. H.   That's part of it.

B. B.   I believe I have had a variety of "unposthumous" experiences, all of them certified. I translated an anthological selection of Rafael Alberti for the University of California Press and have a kind of illustrated scroll of merit covered with doves and Andalusian promises in the special calligraphy of the poet to show for it. I translated a good part of the *Cántico* by

Jorge Guillén, and had the pleasure of reading with him jointly at Bennington. He was good enough to fill fly-leaves of my copy of *Cántico* with translations of his own—Wallace Stevens, Joyce, Eliot—instead of doves and calligraphy. That translation, by the way, was done with the "midwifery" of Norman Thomas di Giovanni, who was endlessly self-effacing and sedulous as an intermediary between translators and the poet: a permutation we haven't really talked about as yet. There, the English was discussed in considerable detail by both Guillén and di Giovanni. We all revised and re-revised, until there was a kind of despairing agreement, or its English equivalent, on the text which was to stand next to the Spanish. The same was true of di Giovanni's later project on Borges, for which I was also enlisted. In the case of Borges, we *slaved* at a very special genre of translation that Borges had in mind as par for his course. Of course, Borges knows *better* English-English than we do, and certainly in other ways than we do—down to its Anglo-Saxon marrow, which he especially coveted in exchange for the Latinate marrow of his own language. In the case of Borges, there was a change in the matrices of the two languages, as though he were subjecting the weight and the temper of a Spanish which he regarded as jejune, to an Anglo-Saxon decantation. If Borges had had his way—and he generally did—all polysyllables would have been replaced by monosyllables, especially in the third and fourth revisions, to which he often pressed his absent collaborators. People concerned about the legitimacy of the literal might well be scandalized by his mania for dehispanization.

E. H. He was using you as writing hands . . .

B. B. "Simplify me. Modify me. Make me stark. My language often embarrasses me. It's too youthful, too Latinate. I love Anglo-Saxon. I want the wiry, minimal sound. I want monosyllables. I want the power of Cynewulf, Beowulf, Bede. Make me macho and gaucho and skinny." That sort of thing—though, of course, those were not his actual words!

E. H. Did the period of Borges and di Giovanni follow the Guillén period?

B. B. Yes, by a number of years. Guillén was the first venture involving a stable of translators and a steward. Then di Giovanni undertook a similar venture with Borges—and something very Borgesian happened. First he was devoured by Borges and the cadre of translators he had enlisted to transmit the specifications of Borges. Then, as a result of his proximity to the Master and the indescribable rigors of modifying and leveling the rest of us (for which we all have reason to be grateful), di Giovanni took to practicing the art copiously himself, as Borges' other Other—and outdid us all!

E. H.   A very odd development. I'd like to go back, though, to what we were talking about in connection with your further work—the experience, then, of getting to know Spanish.

B. B.   Well, it's the poets who have a way of making translators out of other poets, and poetry that leads them from one language to another. In my own case, it was Lorca who led me into Spanish—a decade after I had first accepted a translation of him for *The Nation*. Then, ten years later, during a post-war Guggenheim in 1946-'47, while I was at the University of Virginia as loafing poet-in-residence, I took a Spanish course and began to learn the language academically. Then, long before I should have, some would say—before I had brought my literacy to the point where it was theoretically desirable to translate—I simply flung myself at Lorca. I reversed the recommended procedure: I learned Spanish syntax in the act of pursuing the sounds, the idiosyncracies and the poetry of Lorca.

E. H.   Yet you had previously translated Rimbaud with a man who is a master of the subject.

B. B.   I believe I have served under many masters in translating from the Spanish, too—José Montesinos and Luis Monguió of the University of California in Berkeley, Ángel del Río, Paco García Lorca of Columbia among others, as well as the poets themselves—in my encounters with the *duende* of Castilian. All have served as consultants, mediators, trouble-shooters, editors. But I was at first quite solitary with the Lorca—with Lorca and the whole of Mexico, which I visited year after year, long before I made it to Spain, in those winter recesses conveniently provided by Bennington, to get the whole ambience of the language. I combined every conceivable form of circulation and ventilation of the language and the literature, tunneled in every conceivable direction to accelerate my faculty for using the language and calibrate my liberties.

E. H.   It was Lorca himself, the poetry of Lorca, rather than Spanish poetry as a whole . . .

B. B.   Lorca only.

E. H.   I believe your translation of Lorca's *Poet in New York* is dated 1955 and has since appeared in eighteen printings.

B. B.   There's a connection between my apprentice years in Lorca and *The Poet in New York* which I should mention. Donald Allen, then of Grove Press, had read my translations in *Quarterly Review of Literature* and was the first to approach me with the idea of translating the whole of the *Poeta* for Grove Press. It seemed to me a reckless undertaking for everyone concerned, but in the end I said, "Why not?" I was enlisted to translate *Poet in New York* by a man who had the wit and uncanny facility of sensing what are generally called "vogues" or waves in the making, and later turn out to be total landslides of taste—like his later anthology of the "poets since 1945" and canonization of Ginsberg.

E. H.   If I recall correctly, Rolfe Humphries' translation in this country preceded the first edition of Bergamín in Mexico.

B. B.   By a nose, I believe: both should be postmarked about 1940. The long story of the search for a canon for *Poet in New York* and its relation to the scenario provided by Humphries in his persevering and indispensable edition, is enormously complicated and still in search of a conclusion. There is a detailed Chronology in my own edition for Grove, and the transaction is now being reexamined by a cadre of French, Italian, and Spanish Hispanists in Madrid, whose job it is to invent an authorized text for all of Lorca. At the same time, it has been turned into a tour de force of detection by Daniel Eisenburg, a young scholar working against the international grain from Florida State University.* I soon saw that the job of piecing together the potsherds in Mexico and the United States for a provisional text was also inseparable from the ordeal of translating it.

---

*Professor Eisenberg's study has recently been published in a Spanish translation under the title of *"Poeta en Nueva York": historia y problemas de un texto de Lorca*, Editorial Ariel, Barcelona/Caracas/México, 1976, pp 222. A study of similar dimensions was published in Italian (*"Poeta en Nueva York" di Federico García Lorca*, by Piero Menarini), La Nuova Italia Editrice, Florence, 1975, pp. 222.

E. H.   Are you satisfied that you came close?

B. B.   A number of poems still remain to be fixed in the canon, either by fiat from Madrid and Rome, or by maverick scholars, like Eisenberg. To the very last moment of publication, "New York poems," lost, purloined, apocryphal, or hoarded by their possessive and unpredictable custodians, continued to turn up in odd places, like Mallorca. I especially remember a sophisticated bookstore on Calle Madero where I routinely asked for South American books about Lorca, and was told: "We have some copies of the original Mexican edition of *Poeta en Nueva York* on hand." Just imagine! Stored away in that bookstore there must have been some thirty or forty copies of the Editorial Séneca edition of the *Poeta*—retired, rather than remaindered, because of vanished Mexican interest and the apathy of everyone concerned! Such are the adventures of canon-makers who turn up at the right time and get lucky!

E. H.   All very interesting. As before, when we were talking about the translations of Rimbaud and you mentioned Hart Crane, another bell struck; because I'd always thought of Hart Crane as the nodal center in the development of modern poetry, someone very significant, especially for the people starting to write in that period. That is, Crane stands with Pound and Eliot as one of the chief transmitters of European traditions, however imperfectly.

B. B.   However, we all know now that Crane was semi-literate in those languages himself and lacked the sophistication of mentors like Allen Tate and Yvor Winters, who could have taken him to the sources, as Wallace Fowlie took me. There was that linguistic and intuitional seepage, though, that blood-letting; and that was enough for Crane. I mean his capacity to devour, his gusto, his faith in the pleasure principle: all operated like Braille, as a tactile accelerator of good things.

E. H.   With Lorca, we have to do with the happenstance of a Spanish poet writing a totally aberrant work about New York, a city which he inhabited with Crane in 1929, without ever crossing the path of the author of *The Bridge*. A strange situation—a European infusion concentrating on urban life in a way that rediscovered New York to the New Yorkers and surrealism for a displaced Andalusian.

B. B.   Like New York's gift of Washington Irving to the Alhambra and the Caliphate of Granada!

E. H.   Don't you think Lorca's surrealism is the definitive development of his late phase—both the *Poet in New York*, and those last—and "lost"— plays?

B. B.   Certainly it was a timely antidote for that provincial *gitanismo* that enchanted Lorquistas all over the world and drove Lorca himself to surrealist despair. His surrealism was traumatic, if not definitive. But I think it is also related to other trends on the way out; because, perhaps, of new trends pressing toward the center from the periphery, searching for hot-spots: people like Crane.

E. H.   Yes. Also the whole phenomenon has changed with regard to Latin America. You, for example, went ahead to Pablo Neruda after Lorca —a continuity totally understandable in terms of subsequent developments. What I'm trying to get at is that you, in your experience, career, and craft as a poet and translator, have not only incorporated poets in Spanish, but also started something of a trend in English. You made tracks in which others have followed, like it or not.

B. B.   I sometimes flinch at the consequences. Not long ago, I heard from a graduate student in English at the University of California at Berkeley who thought Ginsberg and the San Francisco sound were the summit of all American modernity. He was, if I remember correctly, in the process of completing a history of the poetry of the San Francisco Bay Area from 1940 to 1955 for his doctoral dissertation, and had already interviewed Robert Duncan, Josephine Miles, Kenneth Rexroth, William Everson, and Ferlinghetti, among others far better informed than I. He was perfectly certain in his own mind that my translation of *Poet in New York* was the *swinger* that had set Ginsberg off, and then lit up the whole Western Seaboard like a switchboard.* I wrote him back denying it as

---

*From a letter of March 14, 1973, F.J.C.: "What struck me upon first reading your translation of *Lorca's Poet in New York* was its similarity in attitude, voice, rhythm, imagery, word choice and total effect to Ginsberg's *Howl* . . . Your translation came out in the same year, and I find so many similarities between it and *Howl* that I am almost certain that Ginsberg knew it, that the words were ringing in his head, that you and Lorca were sitting on his shoulder and moving his pen around while he was writing."

icily as I could, hoping it was not so. I haven't heard from him since. He was utterly wishful and tendentious about the whole thing. He found, for example, that the "famous first reading of *Howl* at the now equally famous Six Gallery in San Francisco in 1955" and the publication of *Poet in New York* were almost simultaneous. "Couldn't Ginsberg have read your translations in magazine form?" he wanted to know. Well, he could have —in *Poetry*, *The Virginia Quarterly Review*, *Partisan Review*: but I was adamant and said I didn't think that's what touched off "poetry since '45."

E. H.   Well, there's some strange alchemical transmutation when a "new poetry" arrives at the right time or someone picks up the poet who can transform the whole movement of things: a development vital to the internationalization of poetry.

B. B.   Certainly Neruda believed I was rendering him a cosmopolitan service, and gave me *carte blanche* in the choice and execution of volume after volume, except in the one case when he urged me to share a book with Alastair Reid to blend American translation with British. He even insisted that I was the only one to translate his first and only play into the kind of theater and poetry he intended, while I spent two years debating the same premise with myself. The fact that I undertook the translation of *Joaquín Murieta* can hardly be called a phase in the development of international poetry, however! That was a very personal gamble.

E. H.   But Neruda saw that you were not only doing him a service. You were providing a bridge to North American poetry, as Crane might have wished it to be.

B. B.   Once, Ted Roethke startled me by asking Howard Nemerov to "Tell Belitt that his *Poet in New York* is a kind of Bible to my kids [at the University of Washington]." Was Seattle another phase of the San Francisco backlash, or a plank in the "bridge" of "international" taste?

E. H.   You still translate from the Spanish?

B. B.   Yes, though at this point I prefer to work at more modest jobs. I've just finished translating a volume by an "unknown" Peruvian-Californian who happens to have the endorsement of a preface by Neruda:

Enrique Huaco's *Piel del Tiempo*. In this case, the book was put in my hands by his brother, then Professor of Sociology at Yale, after a joint reading of Neruda by Emir Monegal and myself. I've done a smorgasbord of miscellaneous Spanish talents for magazines like *Mundus Artium*, *Tri-Quarterly*, *Quarterly Review of Literature*, *Salmagundi*, *Poetry*, *Canto*, etc.

E. H.   There have recently appeared other translators of Neruda: a small cadre of them, one might say.

B. B.   That's all to the good. It's what I'd hoped for—many sounds, many orientations and intonations, many biases (though not their accompanying Mafia of vendettas), many permutations of pleasure—a whole orchestra tuning up on processes and procedures. But recent translations have all been on the side of a puristic leveling of Neruda to the lowest case of the literal word. Neruda is sacrosanct to his American idolators. I prefer the "choral" rendering of Neruda because tolerance and abundance are better than authorized or monogamous translation. I deplore all fixed points and terminal goals of translation.

E. H.   When you went to Neruda, did you have to wrench your style—did you have to think of a way of doing it that was different from the way you'd done other poems?

B. B.   I never know how translation ought to be done before I have begun to do it; though the "wrench" was immediately apparent to me. The posture of translation has to be inductive, I think. If the sound is right and carries with it my whole engrossment as a poet, translation has a way of falling into place, in the same way that poems do. I have no program unless it is one of leading naively and obsessively with the whole stock of my resources as a *poet writing poetry*. How else can one survive the punishing trajectory of a whole book which selects the best of four or five volumes at a time for anthological display and delectation—a jolting set of texts, some of which are right for you, others of which are tedious, or with tedious stretches? As a translator in bulk, one must move with the same plausibility through hot and cold, through what is congenial and what's remote, roll with the punches on some least common denominator of continuing energy. One *can't* be Nobody In Particular. I see no other way to do it.

E. H.   You're temperamentally more akin to the lyric poems.

B. B.   Well, politics was never my motive for translating Neruda; and surrealism is not my dish of tea.

E. H.   Those endless pile-ups of metaphors!

B. B.   The metaphors excite me. There's a special magic in the divination of surrealist metaphors—which are really a kind of irrational metaphysics or therapeutic shorthand: like reading entrails or tea-leaves. In the case of *Poet in New York* I found some sections overstated, too facilely or too hysterically surrealist—until I began to read the poem as an irreversible autobiography of alienation, by a poet who exquisitely embodied one culture and was made to collide with its antithesis here. It is a psychological document, an ethnical *pesadilla* whose real passion and significance as an idiom lies in its queasy transcription of horror and loss and panic, without the mediation of prudence, like an inked thumb on a blotter, or an anatomical dye.

E. H.   It's a remarkable poem; and still, perhaps, will never be wholly assimilated; a little like *Song of Myself* (which gets a lot of currency nowadays at universities in a way it never did twenty or thirty years ago) —a poem which is probably about the same length as *Poeta en Nueva York*. Structurally, say—all fifty-two sections of Whitman can be accounted for. I wonder if that will ever happen to the *Poeta*.

B. B.   Let us say that it is the fate of the vanguard always to move to the center; and universities are a vehicle of that movement. At first reading, one feels such poems are always *ahead* of one—that is part of their exasperating attraction: something to be sniffed out, or be shaken by: then a "classic" moves out from under, to become the signature of one's "modernity."

E. H.   But speaking of "psychological documents" and collision courses between Lorca and other cultures barbarous or exotic to him—Madrid or Andalusia of the '20's and Manahatta's Harlem of '29: I wonder what *is* the text actually translated? Put it another way: is the text always a stable quantity, or is it that, plus something else—a variable?

B. B.   I find there are always some parts of a total text which a translator approaches with repugnance, or distaste, or coldness, other parts which appear uncomfortably obsolescent, and others which we can't wait to get to because there is an exhilarating affinity or symbiosis between what comes to us happily and what the text requires of us. Of course, we all have our idiosyncracies, our differentials, our perfect or imperfect equations; but whatever disturbances trouble the surface of translation, the center, which is where the poet lived, must retain its integrity. In the course of translation, I fight fastidiousness: personally, I shrink from diffuseness, wordiness, failures of imaginative tension where a poet like Lorca loses his way while the words accumulate. The longueurs weary me; yet I feel the poems must be rendered *as they are*: those are the rules of the game. However much the original may resist congenial transmutation into one's favorite modality and tone, they must be given safe and passionate passage. Tedium is also part of the game. Professional translators must combine with the alien as well as with the ingratiating and expedient.

E. H.   I notice that in your own translation of *Poet in New York* there are notorious puzzlers which you've translated literally. Doesn't one have to make decisions—

B. B.   One must make command decisions at all points of maximum interpretive traffic. The problem of "ambiguity" is of course a classic one: how to work in a limbo of deliberately enigmatic implications, a crossfire of contexts, and keep ambiguity *ambiguous*. Even there, one makes interpretive or preferential judgments, one uses the tactical cunning of Solomon. That is part of the task of translation. One can't wait in the wings forever, immobilized by the categorical allegiances of the literalist.

E. H.   How would you test whether a work of translation is faithful or has a right to exist in its own terms, whatever its relation to the original work? Is there any test?

B. B.   What is the test for the *Rubaiyat of Omar Khayyam*? Or Pound's *Sextus Propertius*? There is nothing as blue and red as litmus paper. There are signs, *faits accomplis*, reassurances: for one thing, volatility; responsibility, for another, the certainty that all the elements have been subjected to atomic scrutiny—all of the words as they pass from their moorings in the Spanish into the ink of the translation, with no leaps of convenience or deletions such as you might find in the *Imitations* of Lowell.

E. H.   He's taken that word from Dryden, and Dryden means an "adaptation."

B. B.   I've written as curiously as I could on that subject, to explore my own criteria of translation. I've weighed the forfeits of expressive translation against the privations of anonymous translation: "translation as personal mode," against "the translator as nobody in particular." *Both* are ploys, impersonations, heuristic deceptions.

E. H.   Can you go into that further?

B. B.   I would rather let the pieces speak for themselves as I wrote them for *Salmagundi* and *Review '74*, rather than paraphrase off the top of my head. In the case of Lowell's *Imitations* I wanted to consider the kind of option which deliberately subordinates the translated poet to the identity of the translator and in which the intent is, as it were, binaural: to provide two voices for one. Lowell has opted even more flamboyantly for *one* continuous voice, indelibly and conspicuously his own, when he is translating as he pleases from the whole canon of European and Mediterranean masterpieces.

E. H.   Then he amalgamates his translations into the body of his own poetry.

B. B.   I see it as a kind of dramatism—a histrionic or supportive use of "the individual talent" of the original, at a time when, for one reason or another, the poet's initiative has lapsed or sagged or withdrawn to lick its wounds. What follows, I think, is an expedient—a desperate—use of translation to compensate for the translator's blockages: to keep a big talent moving and perform all of the feats which have to do with the whole repertory of poetry, rather than the special register of his own oeuvre. "Translation as trampoline"—or as I suggested in the beginning, a "jungle gym."

E. H. I have two feelings about that, myself: one of them is that Lowell was wrong to do it, because he gave translation a bad reputation at a time when it needed more imaginative support. And he was right to do it because he went way out on a limb and thereby provided a center for corrective discussion and work on the part of other translators at a time when the issues were confused.

B. B. I think that large talents have less choice in such matters than the middling or unharried ones. Lowell's motive was self-preservation, like Hölderlin's, survival rather than charity. I value that enormously.

E. H. But as a practice for others, it has its good and bad sides.

B. B. It does.

E. H. And, as often turns out, the private dilemma of Lowell and Hölderlin has resulted in many good things, in a kind of "pure research" of international and linguistic exchange—including their translations.

B. B. What I try to suggest in my article is that much of what Lowell did was, basically, *translation* in the old-fashioned sense, despite the strange aberrations and gerrymanders which result from jettisoning what was incompatible. In Lowell's case, I yield to the urgency which leads major talents to prey on the identities and styles of other great talents, as an armature for their own utterance. Only think of the many disguises of Blake and Keats for preying on Milton, and Neruda for preying on Whitman!

E. H. I suppose Lowell was doing in his own way what Pope and Dryden were doing with Homer and Virgil in their time. Pumping their own poetic juices—not to mention their prosody!—into the text.

B. B. I think in many ways Lowell is more "faithful" than Pope or Dryden.

E. H. All one can hope to develop is some sense of the immediate goals that are involved *in* translation and *for* translation, quite apart from matters of public benefit or eventual public worth. The fallacy of translation as something which is "deceptive" and a "betrayal" of an original (—*traditore*—we all know the Italian word for it—) can really be understood as part of a creative undertaking—creative, not in the wild sense, though sometimes that is important, too, but as the transfiguring of invention. That seems to have kept *you* working for years!

B.B.   There must be some allowable ambience of *pluralism* in the whole premise of multi-cultural translation.

E.H.   Yes.

B.B.   Personally, I work out of the premise that there is no universal motive, like "fidelity," which all translation should serve. We serve a multiple, and not a univocal, function . . . We translate to accomplish different ends. For the functions do differ. Some translate in order to exist supinely on the opposite side of the page as a trot to pace subservient readers who cannot or will not construe the language and meanings for themselves, or check back with a dictionary and a grammar. Others translate to deepen their own progressive absorption in a sustaining talent: there is a vast body of translation in which the enlightened disclosure of admiration is primary—a kind of substantive embodiment of *praise*. Certainly, the eminent and odd, like Rilke, Pope, Baudelaire, Hölderlin, Marianne Moore, Lowell, have always been allowed their own keyboard and predominant sound.

E.H.   Yes.

B.B.   But the poet who is less than "monumental" himself is an interloper!

E.H.   It's a question of bravura. The actor "interlopes" on the play and people admire the performance because they have come to see the performance, and not because they are calculating "fidelity to Shakespeare" at every stage of the play. The same thing might well work for translation. There are live translators and dead ones, and then there is the over-riding truth that all translation is by nature an obsolescent datum. We all know that translations decay, as styles decay.

B. B.   That's a crucial consideration, I think. One must always translate *inside* the wide-open premise that *re*-translation is always going on. If one realized the poignancy and perishability of all translation, the built-in obsolescence of the search for contemporaneity, the premise of unalterable models like a Newtonian universe or the equation for energy would be scrapped. We would realize that the translator's vocation is a *comic* one. Comic in the sense that he's in an absurd situation in which he begins pietistically with the demure proviso that is part of every translator's apology for his translation: "I'm engaged in what I know is an impossible transaction. Of course, my original was innate to the identity of its creator and the language which embodied it. It is epistemologically and imaginatively irreducible, unrepeatable. It can't be translated." Then one immediately sets about translating it, as if all were really possible: *that's* comic! The critic then adds to the comedy by insisting in advance of the fact that Neruda, let us say, or Lorca, must be present in his own signature, and cannot be simulated; or that his Spanish can never be functionally or prosodically secondary to the translator's English. The original cannot be made to seem to *derive* from the English translation, just as Spanish cannot seem to be a derivative of English. And somewhere, apart from it all, sits the Sphinx of Translation herself, compounding the enigma with a final riddle which dooms positivists and optimists equally: "Your whole posture as a translator is one of systematic abandonment. You are writing in English because you have *forfeited* the language of the original *from the very start*. You cannot therefore expect to recover the truth of the individual talent in a language undreamt of by the poet. What walks on four legs in the morning, on two in the noon, and on three in the total darkness of composition, is Translation."

E. H.   What would you say to the metaphor of a pianist playing Chopin, as another permutation? Isn't he translating?

B. B.   What would you say to Rimsky-Korsakoff's orchestration of Moussorgsky's *Boris Godunov*?

E. H.   We may have all been too exclusive, puristic, blind, in our view of what originality always and only is. That may be at the source of our prejudice not only against certain translators and their work, but against the whole notion of translation as a "discipline." As you say, there's a certain daring and absurdity translators invite which others find—

B. B.   That dilemma of absurdity! All translators knowingly participate in it, all openly confess it: it is one of the hazards of the occupation. Yet still the purists bear down on the translator as though translation had no right to be what Neruda expressly claimed for his own poetry: *impure*, fallible. And still the translator plaintively explains: but I am only trying to bring back Neruda and survive!

E. H.   It's a strange duplicity that works against the person who's trying to rescue something called pleasure and ally it to meaning and genius. What the critic does is say: This man is doing a very bad job of rendering something which I know exists in the original in a different way. *Traditore!* But the critic is able to say that only because the translator has accepted the comedy, as you put it, with the seriousness of all true comedians, and has made possible something which would have never existed if he had adopted the obvious and meaningless pieties: "This can't be accepted as the original."

B. B.   Otherwise the whole phenomenon of translation would be immobilized in the wilderness of "duplicity."

E. H.   Exactly.

B. B.   Or all language would lead us back to Bedlam or Babel again. No. There must be a workable dissemination of the world's avowedly irrecoverable originals. There must be a responsible tolerance and curiosity —a *skepticism*—regarding the ways in which *all* translation may happen, in the search for a shared humanity.

E. H.   Your word, "pluralism," can stand as a motto for what is needed Not only a variety of translators and styles, but a sense that, whatever the relationship is, it must take place with more figures than a one-to-one equivalence.

B. B. It is very enlightening for translators to *be* translated in kind—like the therapy of psycho-analysis is first made to rebound on the potential psychiatrist, in his pursuit of the analysand. I often wish that on all literalists. There's nothing more depressing than an over-awed literalist at work on your own poetry. Whenever my verse is translated by others, I leave a long, loose rein and urge translators to follow some powerful lead of their own: to put their poem together from beginning to end and calculate the thrusts on their own momentum, to find a brio which guarantees a continuum *for them* as well as for me. At times I have been led to approximate or *revise myself* in the Spanish of some inadequate translation —to *make up* in Spanish something I did not write originally, as the only way out of my own English. Having tried on that shoe, I'm more convinced than ever of my jittery stock of "premises." No one is more tolerant of a translation, I've found, than the poet translated. He is the first to disbelieve in the whole venture, and marvel at all the salvage. *"Of course* you can't do what I do, as I have done it! How perfectly extraordinary that you get anything accomplished at all! Just give me a little character, for heaven's sake! Just bring me back alive! Make readers pay attention and follow through. Be imaginative. Write as well as you can." *He* gets the comedy! Imagination isn't a phenomenon that can be limited to the poem in its original state. As a translator, it is legitimate, it is imperative, to work imaginatively, joyfully, energetically, ingeniously, patiently, inventively, yourself. Imagination cannot be present in the original only, and absent from the equivalence. The very notion of "equivalence" is an imaginative one.

E. H. And of course, imagination is the most—

B. B. —most risky and most daring, the most desired and mistrusted faculty: the most dangerous. We mistrust it but we can't renounce it. How can we afford to renounce imagination in the midst of a process we know to be absurd and inimitable? Or avoid saying to ourselves, in the awful solitude of translation, with an upbeat of nausea and wonder: "Well, I don't know for a *fact* what the poet knew, but I believe I can *imagine* how this might sound in my language." That's an honest and poignant transaction.

E. H. John Hollander said that the theory of translation must involve a theory of literature; that when you talk about translation you have to assume there are readers willing to play the game.

B. B.   Exactly so. Who would deny a poet the risks and the pleasures of the imagination at every stage of the process that produced the poem? How can a translator assume that the poet has "*done* all that *for* me" in advance of the translation and then block his passage through minds and languages surrogate to his own? Only in imagination—here's Keats again! —does the translator wake up, like the poet, and find all is "true," as in Adam's dream.

E. H.   Have you ever written a poem based on a poem in Spanish but which, say, you don't have at hand and which you're not at the moment thinking of as a translation?

B. B.   Now that's a very curious question! There are translations "after" the poets they invoke—long after! At times I am paid the lethal compliment of being found "better than the original," whatever that is. I wince at that; but I understand how such delusions arise, out of the translator's need to explain and complete meanings, as well as report them—meanings which need never be *chosen* in the original language precisely because they have accommodated themselves to that language—forcing the critic's choices upon the poet.

E. H.   Isn't it a large-mindedness we hope for from the reader?

B. B.   It's curiosity I ask for—basic curiosity: what Kierkegaard called the "infinite interest in realities not one's own." In so far as the original text has been touched by the imagination and the language imposed by the translator remains an equivalence, there can never be a definitive text —that is another part of the comedy and another part of the forest. Even in the original, the meanings will always be viewed at different angles and in different ways by different critics, different centuries, different encounters. There is no single, originating, authentic locus of all meanings. A poem is an *area*, a quantum rather than a datum. It's an artifact, too—yes —but the artifact is what one can never wholly repossess: it remains unique to the language and the mind that puts it together, and keeps aloof. Everything else is apocryphal. I'm perfectly willing to live with that, and dowse my way through a world of equivalences. Translation forces ambiguity upon one. It is up to the translator to enjoy the *nausée* of ambiguity and use it in objective and visceral ways to assemble an ambiguous circumstance: the co-existence of two improvising identities touching each other in equal but alien ways for purposes of imagination and pleasure. One can never hope for terminal completions. Nothing has been terminated. All is yet to come: readers and critics are already at work construing the experience differently. No one concludes the translation of a poem, any more than one concludes the reading of the original.

E. H.   Well, that's a principle I find very useful, helpful, and resolving.

B. B.   However, the translator has to *live*; he has to stay alive while handling the disintegrating energy of identities other and more powerful than his own, or be demolished by them. I'm not talking about the purely "occasional" translator who can afford to be categorical because all he will ever take on are isolated pieces, rather than whole books. What is dismaying, is the volume confronted *from beginning to end*: "You mean to say I have to translate *everything*?" "Yes, everything."

E. H.   "Eat every drop on your plate!" Who's to say that?

B. B.   I must say that to myself—and move through all of it, every bit of it, with the same appearance of consanguinity.

E. H.   Exactly. You make a very strong case for what you actually do as a translator, and that's exactly what I was hoping for in talking with you.

B. B.   But one thing I'm convinced of, after having written a great number of prefaces, none of which has been read by reviewers or critics: translation is a provisional art. All my premises are provisional. I ask to be judged in terms of what I initially set out to do and what I initially concede you cannot expect of me.

E. H.   The translation exists somewhere between the translator, as the maker of a provisional text, and the original text itself, which seems to be a variable quantity and quality—sometimes non-existent, as they say in the case of oral epic poems or ballads, or even, let's say, Auden's oeuvre, after he decided he was going to change his earlier published poems because they no longer coincided with his beliefs, and he was embarrassed by them, like Borges. That means, as you have already suggested, that the so-called canon of a work is not something you can establish once and for all. This is an important aspect of the question of *"what* the translator translates"—how "reliable" and "faithful" he is. You can't expect faithfulness where there's not something to be faithful to: some redoubtable scenario. As you say, there is no single originating source—not even the Mind of God. According to the Cabala, God is Absence.

B.B.   Or floating somewhere in the middle of the air on a visionary bath, or a divan of enigmas. It's the Platonism, the Idea of the Perfect poem, or the Finished Product, the Incorruptible Form that I think interferes with the sweaty labor of translation, the sweaty empiricism in which everything is an action, a commitment, a deed, a choice, and refuses to exist abstractly in the realm of the Potential. One translates as Forster's Professor Godbole prays, singing one's odd little tune and saying: "Come. Come. Come. Come." One has to intrude upon possibility; even the poem speaks in its own right, at its most expressive pitch, as a pure tissue of possibility. The translator provides possibles, probables, utterances, and then tries to anchor the whole floating realm of epistemological possibility. I insist it's an epistemological, rather than a semantic or linguistic, question: *What kind of knowledge does poetry involve?* What is the *thing* that translators can know, and how can their language know it? What is the syntax for its survival as either immediate pleasure or eventual truth? The knowledge must never be falsified: it is a confidence, a trust—but there is a human need to take a stand and mediate knowledge. All translation, at its best, is mediation rather than definition.

E.H.   Then we're back to that question of whether the interpreter is . . .

B.B.   Well, I wasn't thinking in terms of exegetical interpretation alone. In the realm of epistemological discourse, poems exist in order to invite and release inexhaustible probability. Translation should operate with similar exposure to probability. Putting a pulse under your language like tubing for a blood transfusion, working rhythmically and feelingly for the formalization of the forces which give the intentionality of language and sound to the probable—the whole sonal bit—is part of that "knowledge." To what degree can such things be known? How does one consolidate the sonal integrity of a thing in the act of translating it? There's the fascination of translation. On the other hand, one can hardly argue that because a thing is provisional, one has a license, poetic or otherwise, to multiply chaos. But where provisionality abounds (I sound like Saint Paul talking about grace!) the determinations should also abound, or remain suspended and multiple. One is merely faith-full: as faithful as one can be under circumstances which don't moralize as well as, say, dogma does. The operative word is *faith*, and not *fidelity*.

E. H.   You're saying something very interesting to me in connection with the desire of the original poet to express something that, as we all know, never got expressed; or possibly exceeded the poet. When a poet sees a translation of his work, his interest in the poem as a work-in-progress momentarily rekindles. He says to his translator: You go ahead and maybe you'll find . . .

B. B.   That's very true.

E. H.   . . . perhaps what I left out, or what leaped ahead of me. That, I suppose, is another touch of comedy that makes all utterance kin.

B. B.   Something very similar happens to me when a Nerudist or a Lorquist gives me the exegesis of a poem as a track to ride a translation on, or a thread through the maze of impersonated fidelities. I myself remain curious about the thing I *myself* am contriving. I don't know where my labors will take me, and I certainly don't know how the original ought to have been translated, before or after the fact. I take my lumps as a translator, hoping as I go that nothing has really been violated and that the proportions of the original have been maintained even though my own dynamics have merged with the poet's. I wear my conscience where it belongs: at the tip of my pen, and not on my sleeve like a medieval garter. Now the positivist and the literalist work differently. They say: "Look here: the poem is what it is: and what it is, is *this*! Behave yourself! Do as you are told and all will prove cumulatively right because the whole is the sum of its parts, and all the parts are there, by my count." Of course, the translation of scientific discourse, or even fiction, is a different thing. There, functions differ. We are talking about the most elusive and absurd of all ventures in translation—something that is never the sum of its parts: poetry.

E. H.   There are two figures to be mentioned—three, really: Nabokov, Borges, and Beckett. Nabokov and Beckett are probably closer to each other than to Borges—but in the sense of multi-lingual writers, those three are continually confronting their work in terms of what *else* it might be, and, in fact, what it has to become when, say Beckett translates himself into English or French.

B. B.   Yes, that's interesting. They sit in the doorway of Janus, or Tiresias. How does a translator behave when translating *himself* from one "original" to another?

E. H.   He does what any other translator would do, I suspect, even if he were not translating his own work. It's generally considered a bad idea— to translate your own work. Maybe that is the doorway of Narcissus. What he does is to recreate it.

B. B.   And is often "faithless" to his own original!

E. H.   There was someone who hit Lowell over the head—I think it was Daniels in his collection of speeches, *The World of Translation*—for having deliberately misread in his translation a poem of Anna Akhmatova. He infuriated her, accordingly to Daniels—not because of any personal injury, but because she was trying to say something in the poem which had a wide humanistic relevance.

B. B.   Well, we've already ruled out quixotic or capricious substitutions. We've agreed that the poet has a right to protest to his translator (Lord knows about *imitators*!): "You've been close to me all the way so far. You *owe* me . . . "

E. H.   . . . the rules of the game, the ground base." But in line with what you were saying before about Borges—his desire to recast his work by surrogate means, deliberately—

B. B.   I think it was quite proper for Borges to carry his translators into the labyrinth with him, as a comedian rather than a tragedian, and pursue his known curiosity regarding all fictive outcomes—especially "the supreme fiction." His comic stance regarding both the language of his youth and our somber translations of it, had the right ring of sobering facetiousness. He meant it seriously. It is the function of comedy to dwell upon vices, affectations, foibles.

E. H.   But then he wrote the central fable about translation in "Pierre Menard"; so he's a very important sibyl in this whole bilingual mystery.

B. B.   Borges was always the first to question: *Who* is the author of *what* —and for how long? In the same way, it is serious and fruitful to ask: Was Borges the author of di Giovanni—because by some magic known to them both he invaded the identity of di Giovanni and translated them both into Siamese?

E. H.   Again, it's something "histrionic," as you say: a dramatistic use of personae.

B. B.   And a philosophical one. In so far as Borges himself was aware of his equivocations—of originating and repudiating Borges, and then translating him by proxy—he forced the question precisely to the point where it ought to exist for all translators. Mimesis is only one permutation of translation in the long comedy of Languages in Search of an Author. The play is Pirandellesque; but the fiction is Borges' own, just as the double of an apocryphal Juan de Mairena was Machado's.

E. H.   One thinks of all those games with languages by the multilingual poets who could have written the poem in English, but did not: Nabokov, Borges, Beckett—

B. B.   And a few who did, like young Huaco. But it is Borges who makes the real point and haunts us forever after—that language in itself is provisional; only Borges, who has seen the emperor naked under his verbal clothing. It's Borges who tells us the translator has a responsibility to provisionality—that he must draw needle and thread through an invisible cloth, work without a false sense of having somehow *circumvented* the provisional in the act of translation, or having completed the poet in a way that the poet himself did not. It's translators and critics who dream of completion and the literal, and the poets who say: "Adieu! The Fancy cannot cheat herself so well/As she is famed to do!" In this sense the translation of poetry can never exceed the enigma of it, and be true.

E. H.   The play's the thing: the interplay.

B. B.   From *ludere*: to play; or *interludium*: the play in between the play. All translation is ludic, before it is ethical. It turns into "play" the moment one moves out of the language of the original—the most serious play imaginable, since all knowledge hangs in the balance, or waits in the wings: the play of language with language, and possibility with utterance.

E. H.   Very good.

B. B.   Why not leave it at that? Much good will come of it, as Howard Nemerov, who once called translation a "desperate system of double entry bookkeeping," or something close to that, likes to say enigmatically.

E. H.   The good of unused distance? Of detachment?

B. B.   The good of playing the game like a true gambler, for risk and pleasure. The good of chastening misgiving.

E. H.   Well, perhaps the best place to conclude a conversation about poetry and translation is with a novel of Melville's—who was no slouch at. enigmas himself. *The Confidence Man*, which I've always thought his best work, ends, I believe: "Something more will come of this masquerade."

B. B.   That's the tone. Confidence is the name of the game.

II

Prefaces to Translation:

Theory

Pleasure first—
then truth!

1

The Translator as Nobody in Particular

A ny bilingual translation of the complete text* of *Residence On Earth* is so crucial an occasion for the canon of Pablo Neruda in this country that it might almost be termed a liberation. It delivers a talent, Homeric in its vision of a continent and a cosmos, from anthologists (like myself) who have been preparing the way by mapping the relative densities and dimensions of the poet's itinerary during five prodigious decades of spiritual wandering. Presumably, it restores the poet *intact*—with his longueurs, his obsessions, his idiosyncracies, and his native language— and compels the reader to inhabit the *time*, as well as the continuum, of a singular commitment, without abridgement or intervention. It also presents us with an artifact in English in which the translator professes to "as much fidelity to the author's words and intent as is permitted by the difference between the two languages," and requires us to weigh that against its original.

What does one have when one has a "literal" translation of *Residence On Earth*? The question is a haunting one for poetry, with a history which concerns not only the "fidelities" of Mr. Walsh's reading of Neruda's *Residencias*, but the semantics of translation as such. Ideally put, the question is not: How I Sat Down to Translate the *Residencias*, or even a method and esthetic of translating Neruda, but whether, in the words of Saint Paul, "there be *knowledge*": what needs to be known by reader and translator alike, and the extent to which it is knowable. Ideally answered, the question would engage the poetics, linguistics, and epistemology of translation, as well as the particulars of two texts confronting each other *en face*, across the binder's seam. At its most squalid, the occasion could

*Residence On Earth *(Residencia en la tierra)*, Pablo Neruda. Translated by Donald D. Walsh. New Directions, 1973.

descend to the level of a cockfight or a provincial *alternativa* between literalist and liberalist—a trading of readings in which two irreconcilable premises devour one another and nothing is left but the sneer on the face of the Sphinx.

Let me say what I can regarding the epistemology of "literal" translation and its consequences for the truth of the *Residencias*. "Truth" of translation, "accuracy" of translation, or, in the moralized jargon of the trade, "fidelity" of translation, are generally assumed to be cognate with the practices of the sedulous literalist. Indeed, the effect of matching simultaneously printed texts in parallel columns is to induce a positivism with regard to poetry and the imaginative transfer of languages that is both misleading and illusory. It assumes, in the first place, that the original itself is knowable in a version which is innately and univocally available to all, as a kind of *datum-an-Sich* which should induce all responsible translators to render the poet's paradigm in identical terms. Its attitude toward the dynamics of language itself—toward the behavior of one verbal symbol in relation to another, and their outcome—follows a premise of scientific optimism which even the sciences have come to outgrow. In the romantic pattern of the "microbe-hunter," the literal translator would take his foreign text into the laboratory of the pure scientist, subject it to a science of absolute communication, a semantic bombardment of its fissionable phonemes, and emerge with basic transmutations into English. A simplistic semantics and a misguided analogy with scientific method have led him to identify the truth of a poem substantively with its "words," and its "intent" with its data. Yet the "science" of translation is often no better than a science-fiction of translation, and the weapon of "accuracy" merely a magical change of clothing, in which the mild-mannered reporter emerges from the telephone booth minus his specific gravity, in the accoutrements of the Superman.

There will be few to question the premise that a poem is made up— apparently—out of words, as a truth is made up out of "facts"; but a collection of facts does not constitute a truth, and a collection of words does not constitute a poem. It is the *relationship* between facts that determines a truth, and the relationship between words—sonal, formal, textural, affective, latent, asseverative—that determines a poem. Coleridge would say that in the beginning was a *passion* rather than a word; and that the source of all poetics is properly a "balance in the mind effected by that spontaneous effort which strives to hold in check the workings of passion

. . . consciously and for the foreseen purpose of *pleasure*." It is to this relationship that the translator of poetry addresses himself—a relationship which he soon discovers does not gratuitously spring into place, as an effect follows its cause, once the English word has followed "literally" upon the Spanish. A fine translation is not a Rosetta Stone decoded, but always has something confidential about it.

Certainly literal translation has a right to exist along with all the other fictions and ploys of the translator: mimicry, superimposition, imitations, equivalences, mouth-to-mouth resuscitation, and lexicographical and syntactical "high-fidelity." All partake of the gift of tongues, all are part of the hubbub. All have their pieties, their shortcomings, their bigotries. In the case of *Residence On Earth*, however, the search for criteria is haunted by another factor which compounds the enigma: the poet's choice of an irrational medium in which words no longer offer guarantees of "intent," and intents are no longer "normative commodities" accessible through systematic transliteration. I refer to the celebrated "surrealism" of the poet's address: a "tormented poetry" in the words of Amado Alonso, in which "poetic meanings subjectively intuited do not disclose themselves as nameable and describable things, but through the mediation of images and metaphors—that is to say, slices of reality constructed *ad hoc* by the poet and valid only as symbols, indirect expressions of affective intuitions."

Here, at least, it would appear that the literalist's tactic of fingering the upraised *words* of the original like a kind of Braille in the total blindness of poetry, might offer an alternative to the overawed translator. It is the procedure preferred by Mr. Walsh—a kind of hard-core stenography described by himself as "transparent," in which the poet writing in Spanish achieves the impossible feat of "speaking for *himself* in a new tongue." Of course, the poet speaks for himself only once—in the tongue which anchors his psyche and his syntax to the language of the original. His only mode of existence, is the mode of the original: everything else is apocryphal. Antonio Machado, a teacher of French as well as a poet writing in the language of Neruda, has said that "The only living language is the language in which we think and have our being. We are given only one . . . we must content ourselves with the surfaces, grammatical and literary of all the others." Similarly, the translator, on the other side of the binder's seam, is forced to confront the alienation of his own tongue and speak for its character as a process commensurate with the original: he can never be diaphanous. The binder's seam is there to remind us that the translation of poetry is not a systematic plagiarism of the original, under cover of a second language: it is an act of imagination forced upon one by the impossibility of the literal transference or coincidence of two languages, two minds, and two identities, and by the autonomy of the poetic process.

The role of "being nobody in particular" is the least interesting of the available roles of the translator of poetry. But does it nevertheless *work*? To return to the question originally proposed: What does one have when one has a literal translation of *Residence On Earth*? In the first place, one would have to say that instead of "transparency" or fidelity, one has a usable, if sanctimonious, opacity. We have a venture of conspicuous diligence and good conscience which holds the whole of a baffling undertaking to its course, pursues its literal bias with only occasional lapses into presumption, and registers its reading not so much on the other side of the binder's seam, as in the spaces over the Spanish reserved for the undergraduate trot rather than the "poem itself." We have, that is to say, a kind of English "kenning," or dubbing, or *skinning* of the poem—the disengagement of a verbal epidermis to suggest the total integument in which the poet's discourse was initially embodied, like the bladder for a metaphysical blood pudding. The accomplishment ought not to be underestimated. In so far as the Spanish words are *there*, we need to know what would happen if they were transposed in a kind of basic English resolutely committed to a premise of anonymous deference, thought by the translator to constitute the morality of his whole enterprise. Not only do we have a total surface which directs us undemonstratively to the depths— the skin for a musculature present only in the organic transactions of the original—but we have a resolute continuity of scale which suggests at least that the translator was faithful to *himself*. Unlike more fanciful translators who often deviate into literalism, Mr. Walsh rarely ventures a chary or a whimsical reading. Indeed, it becomes a kind of event when Mr. Walsh, breaking the lock-step of literalism, renders *"el vendido"* (the sell-out) as "the Judas"; *"diamante"* (diamond) as "flaming jewel"; *"el funesto alegórico"* (the somberly allegorical) as "the metaphorical doom"; or mistakenly turns *"mi sangre"* (my blood) into "my brow," and *"alegres disparos"* (happy explosions) into "gay nonsense" (*sic*). One wonders whatever possessed him. He is not curious or tentative or reversible. For Mr. Walsh, there is no nonsense or misgiving about the moving of the verbal counters, even when the poet himself, midway in a poem called *"Arte Poética"* questions whether all might be rendered "possibly in another even less melancholy way," and alludes to a "swarm of objects that call without being answered," a *"nombre confuso"* (a jumbled name)—which, through another mishap, Walsh has rendered as *"hombre confuso,"* "a bewildered man."

We have, in short, another kind of "equivalence," as the freer modes of translation are generally said to give us equivalences rather than literal equations—a body of information useful to readers and clerks, who may choose to remain ungratified. It is the helpful function of Mr. Walsh's translation to show us how shallowly we have penetrated into the imaginative retrieval of a poem by a policy of abstemious literalism. In the realm of pure research, it leaves us surveying the undoing of creation, like Michelangelo in *The Last Judgment* with his own autographed skin in his hand: a posture important for eschatology, and the comic distance essential to humane translation.

Nevertheless, in a way which is the by-product of the awesome scale of the original itself, it *does really work*. Parsimony, in the face of so many temptations, becomes a kind of saintliness. Prolonged exposure to the English of Mr. Walsh, without the stereophonic distractions of the original, creates a *patois* of its own—a monaural pick-up of the explosive changes of texture and pulse of the original and a metronomic leveling of the full orchestration. All remains predictably bleak, while the Spanish goes on being unpredictably shaken by seismic changes of intensity and direction in the volcanic interiors of the imaginative process. For a time one is almost ready to suspend the admonition of Nerudists like Amado Alonso that: "To understand and savor the poetry of Pablo Neruda, it will not do to first understand intellectually the external constructions and then penetrate to the feelings by this means, but quite the reverse . . . one must first engage the affective climate that is the spirit of this poetry, submit to the contagious suggestivity of the images encountered, to the insistence of the poet's motivation and the sure power of the sonorous constructions." Reconnoitering on the short leash of the literalist, one forgets that the nonesuch English of "I ceaseless from clothes to clothes come sleeping from far away" is a sophomore's parody of Spanish; that in English one does not "weep with health, with onion, with bee"; that only Emily Dickinson dared speak of "each invisible water" in sober earnest. At other times, the entrapments of a chicano syntax and word order seem

more incorrigible and ungainly: "in my guitar interior" for—of course!—
"en mi interior de guitarra," or "It's not true so much shadow upon your
hair" for the Spanish underpinning: *"No es verdad tanta sombra en tus
cabellos."* The latter, carried into a further stanza, turns into a tone-
deafening disaster:

> It's not true so much shadow pursuing you,
> it's not true so many dead swallows,
> so much region dark with laments:
>   you come flying.

Even at the moments when the language is most molten with direct,
psychological discharges, the low frequency of the literalist produces an
obsequious jargon that sets one's teeth on edge; Mr. Walsh comes limping:

> You my enemy of so much sleep broken
> just
> like bristly plants of glass, like bells
> destroyed menacingly, as much as shots
> of black ivy in the midst of perfume . . .
> If there is someone that pierces
> a wall with circles of phosphorus
> and wounds the center of some sweet
> members
> and bites each leaf of a forest giving shouts
> I too have your bloody firefly eyes
> and can impregnate and cross through the
>   knees . . .

Certainly, this is not the voice of Pablo Neruda "speaking for himself
in a new tongue"; it is not even the voice of Donald Walsh speaking out of
Madison, Connecticut. It is only literalism at its most supine and myopic,
reaping the wages of anonymity: a translator's option of poverty, chastity,
and obedience transposed into a crucifixion of self-abnegation. If the
whole text persisted in this vein of jaw-breaking asceticism, we would
have to dismiss the venture of a "literal" translation of *Residence On Earth* as
a catastrophe for poetry. More often than not, however, Mr. Walsh steers
an intelligible if uneventful course, provides acceptable readings, and
works within the syntax and inflection of an English with which we can
basically concur. Significantly, it is in the *Third Residence*, devoted to
categorical denunciations and invective—the essentially assertive discourse

of a patriot and the propagandist—that the literal yield is most productive and the language most plausible. Mr. Walsh's translation of the anathemas of "Almería" or the eulogies of "Antitankers" leaves no bubbles between the literal English and the passion of the speaker: direct translation is functionally appropriate, and anonymity is no longer equivalent to anemia. The effect, for once, is visceral. The distinction is an important one, since it helps us distinguish a mode compatible with the literalism of Mr. Walsh, from a modality in which he is likely to appear grotesque and catatonic. Translation is exigent as well as pietistic; and literal translation is especially ill at ease with a poetry where the pressures of language are multiple, disruptive, suspended. It does not cling naturally to the contours with which the syntax and velocities of the original invested its intentions. This is particularly true of the *Residencias*, where the thrust is not merely open, as the mode of Whitman may be said to be open: it yaws in all directions with craters and cicatrices, splinters like shrapnel, makes a fine art of its vertigo. It compels risk, curiosity, impurity, *poetry*.

The fate of a single word—*"ronco"*—may serve to suggest the inertia of the literalist and its consequences for translation. It is a word of considerable character and piquancy in the Spanish: an onomatopoeic adjective to which Neruda is oddly partial in his surreal tilting of the actual. Being an adjective, it is never a substantive entity like a noun: it does not lie flat on the page, or say itself only *once*, like "ball-peen hammer" or "phenolsulfonate." Cassell's Spanish Dictionary will define it for us as "hoarse, husky, rough-voiced," and suggest its proximity to *"roncar"* (snore). Sonally, it relates to the timbre of human and animal utterance, rather than its decibels; nasal, throaty, gutteral, gutsy. Its range throughout the *Residencias* is curiously nonrepresentational: we have *ronco cerezo*, *ronco paso*, *roncas bocinas*, *canto ronco*, *roncas gargantas*, *ronco arbol*, *ronca aguja*, *ronca cesta*, *ronco peciolo*, *roncos rayos*, etc. etc.: cherry trees, footsteps, horns, songs, throats, trees, needles, baskets, leaf-stalks, rays or stripes—all are *ronco* in the encompassing obliquities of Neruda. All force us to wonder about their place in a spectrum of contexts and synonyms. Mr. Walsh, however, is not bemused. In every case his English falls heavily like a brand on a maverick. He says: *"raucous,"* from one end of the book to the other, as though he were in possession of some universal solvent lost to the rest of us.

Actually, of course, he is as much in the dark as any newcomer to the pageants of the surreal: actually, there is no univocal solution, no least common denominator. He is only more cursory and servile. By some law of diminishing returns, moreover, the rigors of the literalist force him constantly to bear witness against himself whenever he is at fault or semantically immobilized. We *know*, for example, that Walsh is wrong when he says "abacus" for *abecedario*, since the former is a device for counting numbers and the latter a primer for spelling words. We know that a sacramental reading of *"licor extremo"* as "extreme unction" (*extremaunción*) is an utterly inappropriate invention; that though a *viejo verde* is a dirty old man there is no reason for assuming that *"cuchillo verde"* (green knife, here rendered as "a sexy (!) knife") has anything to do with dirty old knives; that he has committed howlers in mistaking *"buzos cubiertos de ceniza"* (divers covered with ashes) for *"buhos cubiertos de ceniza"* ("owls covered with ashes"), transliterating *"aguas de espaldas"* as "back waters," and rendering the homicidal humors of *"dar muerte a una monja con un golpe de oreja"* (kill a nun with a punch in the ear) as "slay (!) a nun by striking her with an ear." Similarly we are everywhere aware of inept choices in bizarre contexts to which they could not apply—"surreal" or not. It is plain someone has blundered when *"las dulces tarjetas de larga cola,"* which recalls the lavishly upholstered picture postcards of Neruda's "Poetry and Childhood," turns "sweet cards with long trains" into "sweet calling cards" (*tarjetas de visita*); when *"arañas de mi propriedad"* (spiders of my property) become, of all things, "inherited chandeliers," and a *"golpe de plata"* metamorphoses into "my silver set" (*vajilla de plata*) rather than "a quantity (or windfall?) of money" in downright South American. It is equally obvious that the force of *"documentos disfrutados"* has not been penetrated by calling them "benefited documents," which means nothing at all; and the impersonal grammar of *"sea lo que soy"* which follows unmistakably through the final stanzas of *"Significa sombras"* is badly skewed by replacing the poet's appraisal of his own shadowy obligations with some other shadowy intruder's. And so on.

All this bookkeeping would be secondary, if the mode of the translation had been qualitative rather than categorical: if the translator had given a pulse to his language, a style to his utterance, a point of view to his choices, and held our attention there: if he had, in short, made a poet's demands on the emerging English rather than a pedant's or a proctor in Intermediate Spanish. In the words of Neruda (and Mr. Walsh), it is here that all that is

foreign and hostile begins . . .
the names of the world, the frontier and the remote,
the substantive and the adjectival too great for my heart
originate there with dense and cold constancy.

In the last analysis, the failure of the literalist is a failure of curiosity, nuance, initiative, engagement, *poetry*—a preoccupation with predictable "fidelities" rather than an act of imaginative faith. "To ask with infinite interest," Kierkegaard somewhere says, "about a reality that is not one's own, is faith." In the present case, the faith was little, the interest all too finite and inflexible, and the reality no one's—least of all Pablo Neruda's.

2

Imitations: Translation
As Personal Mode

I t would appear that the domain of Robert Lowell's *Imitations**I would appear that the domain of Robert Lowell's *Imitations** is
public rather than private in character: a "small anthology of European
poetry" from Homer to Pasternak and Montale, drawing upon five languages, including the Russian; with the customary omission of the Spanish. To some extent the concessions to Homer and Sappho are perfunctory:
lip-service to the museum of the Sixth Century B.C., except in some fragments from Sappho which engage Lowell's lifelong preoccupation with
cosmic and personal deprival. As a "small anthology of European poetry,"
however, the collection is obviously sparse and crotchety: what is important is the poet's readiness to explore the European intonation, try the
agonies and the vagaries of the European subject in a way that his American contemporaries have not, and prove them by translation on his
pulses. The effect of his anthology in the long run is to draw the reader's
attention constantly to the person of the translator, and away from the
ambience of "Europe." It would appear that Lowell, like Pound and
Hölderlin, has employed a mode of translation to enact a repertory of
"personae" native to his irascible and inquiring genius; that what we have
is, in fact, not an anthology of European poetry, but a species of dramatism: an artist's mimicry of other artists.

It is Lowell's startling expectation that all—Homer and Sappho, Der
Wilde Alexander and François Villon, Leopardi, Hebel, Heine, Hugo,
Baudelaire, Rimbaud, Mallarmé, Valéry, Rilke, Saba, Ungaretti, Montale, Annensky and Pasternak—"will be read as a sequence, one voice
running through many personalities, contrasts, and repetitions." To this

Imitations, by Robert Lowell, (Farrar, Straus and Giroux, New York, 1961).

end, the mimetic brio of his assault upon the initiating voices is nothing short of ruthless. Sappho has been supplanted by "poems (which) are really new poems based on hers"; Villon has been "stripped"; Hebel has been "taken out of dialect"; Victor Hugo's "Gautier" has been "cut in half"; Mallarmé, Ungaretti, and Rimbaud have been "unclotted" at the translator's pleasure; a third of *Bateau Ivre* has been jettisoned; two stanzas have been added to Rilke's "Roman Sarcophagus": "And so forth! I have dropped lines, moved lines, moved stanzas, changed images, and altered meter and intent."

The scandalized purist need not search long for a vantage point from which to sink his knives where self-righteous pedantry has always found fair game: indeed, Mr. Lowell in his Introduction delivers himself up to would-be assassins with the resolute fatalism of Caesar in the Roman Senate. His admissions and omissions seem almost wilfully suicidal. In that European cemetery of noble utterances and awesome identities which he inhabits, his actions appear vandalous and his appetites necrophilous. The question of Conscience, so touchy to critical moralists, seems never to have occurred to him. What remains is only his need, which is apparently insatiable: to "find ways to make (my originals) ring right for me"; to make Montale "still stronger in free verse"; to "keep something equivalent to the fire and finish of my originals"; to be "reckless with literal meaning" and labor "hard to get the tone"; "to write alive English"; "to rashly try to improve on other translations"; and most significantly, to *keep writing* "from time to time when I was unable to do anything of my own."

Connoisseurs of the translated word have every reason to ask where such wilful gerrymandering may not lead the professed translator: or *why* it is that certain translators translate. Taking Lowell at his own word, one would have to say that the cause is everywhere personal and solipsistic, as well as feral. More than ennui, certainly, must be postulated in his candid admission that he turned to "imitation" when the real thing was for a time denied him and he faced the virility of the world's eloquence "unable to do anything of my own." In the hard school of *"Sauve Qui Peut"* the cannibalism of the large talent at bay must be applauded for finding other means of dining with Landor and with Donne; and I count translation among the most taxing counsels of expedience. It requires, in the first place, an expenditure of self equal to the banquet set forth on the rich man's table. It deploys every skill given the poet's hand in the service of identities and prodigies not his own. As such, it is a form of austerity which emulates the hard morality of Blake: "All Act is Virtue." Incidentally, it also accomplishes a kind of homeopathic therapy for purging past excesses and preparing for exertions yet to come, as when Lowell informs us that his Baudelaire, for all its stunning accomplishment, was "begun as exercises in couplets and quatrains and to get away from the longer, less concentrated problems of translating Racine's *Phédre.*" At its worst, for which Lowell is also accountable, it "imitates" the bittersweet and the mistletoe in its search for symbiotic equivalences, attaching itself to a forest of host-plants to gratify its voracious determination to survive.

This is as much as to say that translation may serve the translator as a form of surrogate identity, as well as a labor of love. In the "parasitology" of translation, it is true, there are certain crustaceans which castrate their hosts, others which attach themselves to large aquatic mammals for the ride and prestige, others which strangle and infect: but the vitalism of Robert Lowell is another thing. I dwell upon it here precisely because his talent is massive enough to invite each of the dangers mentioned, in the service of a commanding identity, and survive. Modesty will get us nowhere in the attempt to arrive at any criteria of translation which may be said to underlie Lowell's accomplishment as intermediary for the European mind. The "one voice" "running through many personalities, contrasts, and repetitions" is unmistakably the voice of Robert Lowell—the most eventful and passionate voice of our epoch, whose voracity matters because it helps to give character to our century. Its impersonations, collapses, reassertions are never parasitical in the morbid sense of enacting flights from the poet's responsibility, or providing lines of least resistance in a peripheral struggle for survival.

On the other hand, little is to be gained from rushing to the defense of the *Imitations* with toplofty disclaimers which pay the poet the dubious compliment of removing him from the imputation of translation entirely. When Professor Alvarez informs prospective readers that the *Imitations* of Robert Lowell is "*not* a book of translation"; that what we have is a "magnificent collection of new poems by Robert Lowell, based on the work of 18 European poets . . . in that constantly expanding imaginative universe in which Lowell orbits," no one is likely to benefit, least of all the translator. Robert Lowell cannot be dismissed as the space-man of recent American translation, circling the European scene in a rubbish of old sandwiches, astronautical weightlessness, and "expanding imagination." Doubtless, he winced, somewhere in the lower gasses, to find his "small anthology of European poetry" hyperbolized as "the most varied and moving book that this leader of mid-century poetry has yet produced" and "oddly, one of the most original." Edmund Wilson's equivocation is not much better: that the *Imitations* is probably "the only book of its kind in literature," whatever that happens to be. Nor can I, despite my mistrust of literalists dedicated to the subversion of inquiry and realism in translation, call the "complaint that Lowell has not followed Baudelaire literally" an "absurd" one, with Mr. Wilson. The gift of absurdity is precisely what the literalist has not got; and it is possible that absurdity may do more than sanctimony to justify the deeper claim on our imagination for the passionate integrity of utterance which characterizes the finest of Lowell's "imitations."

What must be asked in the long empirical run is another question: what are we to understand by "imitation"? Precisely what or who is being imitated in the *Imitations*—Robert Lowell? his great originals? or "due process of translation?" Is the essential premise of imitation: (1) "I will now proceed to English this poem *as though I were* translating it"; or (2) "I will now English this poem as though it were part of my own sensibility, moving from element to element inside my own identity rather than the translator's, assembling and disassembling all inside my own nervous system, committed at all points to my own language rather than the language of the original?" Does the "imitator" differ from the "translator" in that he performs as a kind of versifying dowser, sensitive to the indicated pulls of a *terra incognita*, and capable of turning all into *faits accomplis* of prosody? Is he a virtuoso asked to re-invent at second or third or fourth-hand (at times he has no direct access to the language of the original) the occasion that was uniquely the poet's and the habits of mind and language that originally invested it? Are we concerned with fabrication rather than *mimesis*?

Current practice has no easy answers to these questions, and none is forthcoming in the term given the reader by Lowell. The word itself—imitation—has a notorious history of private and public misdemeanors from its awesome beginnings in Aristotle, up to the present. Life has been "imitated," Nature has been "imitated," Action has been "imitated," with nobody much the wiser. Indeed, the provenance of the "mimetic" factor is almost a certain guarantee of the surrender of the issue to polemical metaphysics and has helped to expose the bias of whole centuries. Thus, one generation talks of copies, phantoms, deceptions, in the name of imitation; another "holds the Mirror up to Nature"; another divinizes its literary models: "To copy Nature is to copy them"; another chooses "the mind's self-experience in the act of thinking" and re-invents Fancy and Imagination. Our own century has benefitted by the combined assaults of I. A. Richards, the debunkers of I. A. Richards, Butcher's preface to the *Poetics*, Francis Fergusson's bid for the "histrionic sensibility," and the long vista of verbal and compositional "dramatism" central to the poetics of Kenneth Burke.

None will serve to crystallize for us the intent of Robert Lowell in this volume. Among more recent symposia on the subject—notably, the barrage of 18 voices out of Harvard *On Translation**—Jackson Mathews' "Third Thoughts on Translating Poetry" comes closest to the issue at hand, in decidedly cautionary terms. "The temptation," he writes, "is much greater in poetry than in prose to fall under the spell of the model, to try to *imitate* its obvious features, even its syntax, or to *mimic* the voice of the other poet. The usual mistake is to believe that the form of the model must somehow be *copied*." The spectrum remains the same—*imitate, mimic, copy*—but the paradox accomplished here is to force Lowell's word to account for all that he has repudiated in the name of "imitation." For whatever its shortcomings, Lowell's *Imitations* is no mocking-bird in an aviary of European originals.

II

Where, then, are we to turn for clues to the criteria of license and translation in Robert Lowell's anthology? In the absence of a "philosophy of composition," I would like to propose a direct reading of the "imitations" into which all has been metamorphosed by the translator himself— a collation of *his* choices, without any hint of paradigms known or imaginable to me, to which they might conform. Among the eerie truths learned by practicing translators is the fact that the One True Translation which all pedants seem to have to hand and consult at will, exists nowhere at all. The particulars of Lowell's originals and the particulars of his "imitations" do exist, however, and together they may help us to construe the personal venture he has undertaken in behalf of his great models. For

*On Translation, ed. Reuben A. Brower (Cambridge, Mass.: Harvard University Press, 1959).

this purpose I have chosen two poems of Eugenio Montale—"Dora Markus" and *"Piccolo Testamento"*—for reasons which seem serviceable enough to me, though I am aware that all acts of translation are unique to themselves, especially where the range of voices and epochs is as orchestral as in Lowell.

Lowell's special fascination with Montale is already apparent in his prefatory remarks on his distinguished contemporary. "I had long been amazed by Montale, but had no idea how he might be worked until I saw that unlike most good poets—Horace and Petrarch are extremes—he was strong in simple prose and could be made stronger in free verse." Here is both the admirer's profession of engrossment in an appealing and powerful talent, and the translator's discovery of a stance from which he might attempt an Archimedean moving of two worlds. Apart from such assurances—which are never idle in Lowell—there are a number of other considerations which confirm the appropriateness of such a choice. Despite Lowell's preference for Baudelaire as a *semblable* in spleen, guilt, and *"l'Inconnu,"* despite his taste for the nostalgias and demoniacal historicity of Rimbaud as an artist *"maudit,"* despite the neoclassical atavisms of Rilke and the delphic contemporaneity of Pasternak which he openly courts, the intonations and textures of Montale perhaps come closest to the temper of Robert Lowell himself. Like Montale, Lowell's prevailing cachet, after *Lord Weary's Castle*, is hard-bitten, melancholy, psychologically dense, with a subject that keeps curiously fluid despite the relentless pressure of despairing intentionality. Poem after poem in *For the Union Dead*, for example, eludes one in the midst of its restless thrust and circuition, as is also the case in Montale's *"Mottetti," "La Casa dei Dognani," "Iride," "La Primavera Hitleriana,"* and countless others. For all Montale's declared predilection for "occasions" (he is content to call a whole volume *Le Occasioni*) what puzzles the reader most in both Montale and Lowell is the nature of the poetic occasion itself: *where* the poem's center was supposed to fall in the midst of the seething interplay of scruples, particulars, recriminations, and insurmountable rejections.

The Italians, with their civilized tolerance of the ineffable, have an admiring word for this phenomenon which they apply like a water-mark to Montale: *hermetic*. The American reader has only the giddy afterthought: but what was it all about? Similarly, both Montale and Lowell carry a dense burden of personal and historical wretchedness, failed loves, psychological landscapes, existential incongruities inseparable from persons and places and electric with the pulsation of the moment. We have the unplumbed exacerbations of Montale's Bellosguardo, Eastbourne, Finistère, Proda di Versilia, to place alongside Lowell's Dunbarton, Nantucket Graveyard, Nautilus Island, Rapallo, and Boston Commons as stations of a spiritual itinerary. Like Lowell, Montale has written a "Ballad in a Clinic," watched storms from "The Coastguard's House," untangled the oddities of a "gnomelike world" from a "Café at Rapallo," scouted the ironies of "A Metropolitan Christmas," turned mordantly upon his own failed purposes in city parks, orchards, on trains and on beaches, leaving an inconclusive savor that troubles the attention without wholly disclosing itself. As in Lowell's volume by that name, a whole genre of heraldic "life studies" is opened up in Montale's "Dora Markus," "To Liuba Leaving," "Arsenio," "Carnival for Gerti," and "Visit to Fadin"; and it is hardly necessary to point out the "confessional" bias of poems like "Little Testament," "Letter Not Written," "Two in Twilight," "To My Mother," and the whole sequence of "Motets." The uncanny impression remains, after many readings of Montale's "Eastbourne," that it is a poem which might well bear the signature of both poets.

As an instance of "life study" Montale's "Dora Markus" is especially noteworthy. Here we have not only "one of the most poignant love elegies of all time" (in the opinion of Glauco Cambon) but a counterplay of intimacy, psychological divination, and the displaced "oriental" mind moving between Porto Corsini and the Austrian Alps. As a study in exile it combines a rich texture of deprival and unrest (*"irrequietudine"*) in a shimmering context of suspended outcomes: the poet's implacable vision of a "voice, legend, destiny" already "exhausted" or manhandled; the *"antica vita"* of a Jewess miraculously surviving from one day to the next by talismanic powers whimsically attributed to an ivory mouse in her jumble of lipstick, powderpuff, nail file; and an immediate scene— majolica interiors, seaside *pensiones*, complete to the bayleaf that "survives for the kitchen." The aim of the poet is, above all, to recover the peculiar *"ansietà d'Oriente"* (Oriental anxiety) at once so fascinating and appalling to the Italian's appetite for melodrama: the capacity of Dora Markus to drift without outcome in a Levantine haze, instead of opting for fatality like a heroine in an opera by Verdi or Puccini.

Formally, it is among the most expansive and readily accessible of Montale's great set-pieces: open, conversational cadences undisturbed by the intrusion of eruptive afterthoughts—the *"dolce stil"* rather than the *"rime aspre"* of Montale's many voices, riding on its phrases, pauses, assonantal depths and graces with an unflinching objectivity. As such, it would not appear to offer the thorny talent of Robert Lowell an ideal vehicle of "imitation"; and it is hard to see how he was persuaded that Montale was either "strong in (the) simple prose of Kay's *Penguin Book of Italian Verse*" or "could be made stronger in free verse." The verse form chosen by Lowell is indeed free to the point of crudity: a prosody without pulse or that factor of inner rhyme which so often limbers the tensions and deepens the resonance of both Montale and Lowell. In comparison with the supple elegance of Montale, it is peculiarly shrill, prosy, angular, without reverberations. Its effect is that of an intermediate, rather than a final, draft, as though Lowell were still mired in the prose of *The Penguin Book of Italian Verse* or preliminary renderings of his own. The presence of Robert Lowell, sometimes playing at "imitation," sometimes pressing for the bare sound and the tough reduction of intricate matters which is his true signature, comes and goes; the equivalences of Montale do not.

Nevertheless, the fact remains that "Dora Markus," for all its ineptitude, is a *translated*, and not an "imitated" poem. Every sequence of Montale's thinking has been retained intact, every image has been confronted, for the most part, in its own context; every effort has been directed with scrupulous and laborious integrity on unfolding the progressions of the poem as they are given the reader by the poet himself—with one maddeningly tone-deaf exception. The last line of all, indispensable to both the pathos and symmetry of the poem—what Sergio Solmi calls "the special curvature of Montale"—weighted with the total charge of Montale's induction of a "voice, legend, destiny," is suppressed: "But it is late, it grows later and later." Characteristically, Lowell has preferred to bleed off into suspension points and ignore the Dantean return to inexorable judgment of the original.

The digressions of Lowell's Montale deserve close scrutiny because they encompass whatever remains of the purely "imitative." It would be pointless and tedious to attempt an exhaustive collation of the two texts, since this is not a study in detection but a glimpse at the propinquities and equivalences of translation. Turning to the most harmless deviations first—the permissible variants or extensions of meaning forced upon the poet by exigency or "inspiration"—one might note the following in the first section of "Dora Markus." A "wooden pier" (*ponte di legno*) becomes a "plank pier": all to the good. The "almost motionless" (*quasi immoti*) fishermen become "dull as blocks"—possibly as extensions of the same plank pier; a "sign of the hand" (*segno della mano*) becomes a Lowellesque "toss of your thumb"; a dockyard (*darsena*) becomes "outlying shipyards" —very Bostonian; what was "shiny" (*lucida*) in Montale becomes "silvered" in Lowell; an impassive spring (*primavera inerte*) is a "depressed spring," and a way of life called "dappled" (*si screzia*) by Montale is curiously "subtilized" in Lowell. In a key-phrase to the poem as a whole, the "soft Oriental anxiety" of Dora Markus is diagnosed by Lowell as "nervous, Levantine anxiety"—and surely "Levantine" is a triumph of the *mot juste*: one of those windfalls of which one says the translator has pinned down what the original could not. The "stormy evenings" (*sere tempestose*), on the other hand, are levelled into "ugly nights," the admittedly equivocal "*dolcezza*" (a word intransigently foreign to English) turns into "ennui" rather than "sweetness" or "blandness"; and the "lake of indifference" (*lago d'indifferenza*) invoked by Montale as the heart of Dora Markus, is modified somewhat myopically into a "puddle of diffidence," as though the word had been read wrongly by the translator.

In most cases, the changes noted are legitimate ventures in interpretation, in which, as Valéry has pointed out, the translator not only presses for language, but "reconstitutes as nearly as possible the *effect* of a certain *cause* (a text in Italian) by means of another *cause* (a text in English)." More arbitrary departures, however, follow fast. Lowell elects to turn the simple "lowlands" or "flatlands" (*bassura*) of Montale into a "patch of town-sick country"—his own invention—and renders "its calms are even rarer" (*i suoi riposi sono anche piu rari*) with the heavy-handed "the let-ups are nonexistent," preempting what the author has left suspended. Other modifications seem merely inept or gratuitous to the quizzical reader: why, for example, "full of amnesia" for "*senza memoria*" (without memory)? Why clutter the "*antica vita*" (old life) of Montale with the needlessly explanatory "old world's way of surviving"?

Similarly, there are some troublesome admixtures of interpretation and fabrication in Part II of "Dora Markus." It is of the essence of Lowell's temperament, and as such, allowable, that the "ragged peaks" or pinnacles (*gl'irti pinnacoli*) of a seascape should turn up as "frowsy shorefront" in Lowell, the geese's cry (*gemiti d'oche*) turn into "catcalls," the "throbbing of motors" (*palpito dei motori*) metamorphose into "the put-put-put of the outboards," American-style, and "the evening that stretches out / over the humid inlet" (*la sera che si protende / sull'umida conca*) contract into "night blanketing / the fogging lake coves." There are also less allowable thrusts, however, which represent not "due process" of interpretation, but random piracies on the part of an "imitator" writing as he pleases, precisely as Lowell declares he intended to. Carinthia "of flowering myrtles and ponds" (*tua Carinzia di mirti fioriti e di stagmi*) takes a curiously baroque turn of fancy: "*Your corsage is the crescent* of hedges of flowering myrtle." Where Dora Markus merely "stoops on the brink" (*china' sul bordo*) Lowell's text explodes roguishly into "sashay on the curb of a stagnant pond"—certainly a strange outburst for the "exhausted" and "indifferent" Dora of Montale's legend. Similarly, there is a revving-up of the "big gold portraits" (*grandi ritratti d'oro*) which preside over her legend, into "ten-inch gold frames / of the grand hotels," as well as their subjects, whose "looks of men / with high (set) weak whiskers" (*quegli sguardi / di uomini che hanno fedine / altere e deboli*) shape up luridly as "the moist lips of sugar daddies / with weak masculine sideburns."

The passages cited, I repeat, constitute passing deflections, digressions, personal readings and renderings of detail; or incidental collapses and fumbled opportunities. Their telltale abundance in the case of "Dora Markus" constitutes a record of imprecision which forces one in the end to dismiss it as inept or provisional; the matrix of Lowell's English text itself, however, remains a *translated* rather than an "imitated" one. As such, "Dora Markus" presents a hard assay that need scandalize no one, however much it may disappoint the admirer of Robert Lowell who *asks* (as would I) for the sound of his voice and delights in following it as an attending presence through the translation it has chosen to inhabit. The failures of touch, the incidental occlusions of intent and tone, the occasional over-acting, over-posturing, over-reaching, the rare pratfalls into prosy approximations, are those of all poet-translators busy at their trade in the ordinary way, probing through that double identity which is the *néant*, the nothingness, from which all true translation begins.

III

Precisely the same must be said for the modality and effect of Lowell's *"Piccolo Testamento"* (Little Testament). Here the translator's total encompassment of his original—his over-all felicity of touch, texture, compositional detail—is as impressive as the botched approximations of "Dora

Markus." Perhaps one ought look no further for causes to such propitious effects, but merely acknowledge their existence as *faits accomplis* and pronounce the union of minds and languages fortunate. The nature of the original, in this case, however, in itself promises more compatible outcomes. In comparison with the pure line of "Dora Markus," the "Little Testament" is a poem more deeply scored with all the idiosyncratic merits of Montale—denser, stranger, nervier in its turns of rhythm and fancy, less immediate in its disclosure of the complex matters touched upon, more obdurate in its hermetic self-scrutiny, more oblique in its confidences. As such, it offers continuous resistance to all that is merely manipulative or "imitative" on the part of the translator and insists on its retention *intact*. At the same time, it is full of glancing turns of direction, texture, metaphorical and stylistic alignment, forging through its transpositions with a driving pulse, without the forfeit of a single misgiving or anxiety.

Presumably, this brings us closer to the vein of Lowell's "Skunk Hour," "Colloquy in Black Rock," "The Flaw," and "The Severed Head": there should be less need, under the circumstances, for the translator to punctuate, revise, delete, and transpose matters to his satisfaction. Deviations from Montale's original persist here as in "Dora Markus," and one might even wonder about the justice of passing incursions. When Lowell gives us a "pearl necklace's snail's trail" for Montale's "snail's trail of mother-of-pearl" (*traccia madreperlacea di lumaca*), the visceral exudation of the snail is falsely represented by a necklace which has nothing to do with the context and omits the special iridescence sought by the poet. Similarly, when Montale, in the "crepuscular" vein of Italian modernism, writes the powder and mirror (*la cipria nello specchietto*) of a lady's compact (probably) into his poem as another instance of talismanic delusion, the poignancy of the ordinary is lost in the "*spectrum* of a pocket-mirror." I see no good reason, moreover, for turning the "soft coal wings" (*l'ali di bitume*) of Montale's descending Lucifer into "hard coal wings," his shadowy Lucifer (*un umbroso Lucifero*) into a "torch-bearing Lucifer," his dance (the "*sardana*") into an "orchestra," even if one grants that the Greek *orxestra* was actually a dancing-place. Lines 5-7, that universal stumbling-stone of translators of the "Little Testament"—and there are many—will of course please no one familiar with the elliptical fascinations of the original, and resists the best efforts of Lowell to improvise on his own. The "light of church or workshop / that neither the black nor the red cleric (acolyte?) / may nurture" (*lume di chiesa o d'officina / che alimenti / chierico rosso, o nero*), breathes heavily in Lowell's version: "The lamp in any church or office / tended by some adolescent altar boy / Communist or Papist, / in black or red." The question of which is the red and which the black, remains, as well as the improbable orthodoxies of the adolescent Communist.

With every allowance made for near misses and far reaches such as these, I should still insist that the "Little Testament" of Lowell's Montale follows through from beginning to end as a *translated* venture of considerable beauty, intact in its own rhythms, illuminations, skills, and integrity: a meeting of minds and imaginations where they intersect in two artifacts—or Valéry's Italian "cause" wedded to his English "effect" which provides the reader, in turn, with a cause in itself. If this metaphysic is too hard or casuistical for the hasty to construe—and I suppose it is—the fault is not wholly Valéry's or Lowell's; or mine. It is part and parcel of a modern semantic bias which expects the croupier's handy transformation of blue chips into cash at the prevailing international exchange at each turn of the translator's wheel. For positivists such as these, the dropsical linguistics of Nabokov's "poetics" is a fitting crucifixion.

Debate on such matters is likely to be bottomless, discussion bad-tempered, and scholarship usurious. I prefer, instead, to dwell on the appropriateness of Lowell's continuing pursuit of translation as personal mode, in the years which have followed his initial *persona* as the castle-bound Lord Weary. Unlike the guerrilla nationalists, professional bridge-blowers, rooftop snipers, and nocturnal infiltrators and assassins of the translator's domain, he has steadily gone on learning his trade by open assault in a variety of skirmishes and full-dress battles, in full view of the enemy, cap-a-pie, in single combat. It is already a very far cry from the glowing fabrications "after Rimbaud," "after Valéry," "after Rilke," in *Lord Weary's Castle*, with their reticent preface: "When I use the word *after* below the title of a poem, what follows is not a translation but an imitation which should be read as though it were an original." The author of *Imitations* and the translator of *Phèdre* and the *Oresteia* need never apologize for poems which presumably "come after" his sumptuous models. His English now lives *simultaneously* with the tongues and talents to which he is beholden.

Similarly, it can be said of his "dramatism" that translation has made it increasingly possible for him to depersonalize his penchant for heroic and patrician *personae* (Jonathan Edwards of the spiders and the "surprising conversions," the memoirs of General Thiebault, the confessions after Sextus Propertius, Valéry, Rimbaud, Rilke, Cobbett—all out of Lord Weary's castle) and move on to the province of drama as such. Here, Lowell's activity has been dazzling in both the pomp and diversity of its passion for transformation. More and more his medium has become theatrical in the literal sense that Lowell has increasingly sought out the provenance of the *played play*, rather than the pirated or inhabited identity of European masters. He has taken a craftsman's pains to "translate" Melville's *Benito Cereno* into an objective theatrical artifact, instead of appropriating the identity of Melville himself. He has translated the *theatre* of Racine, rather than turning Racine into an impersonation of Robert Lowell. More recently he has thrown his total force against the full weight of Aeschylus' *Oresteia* in a bid for total theater.

It is to be hoped that with the passing of time and the channelization of a sensibility which hindsight now shows to have been constantly "histrionic," Lowell will continue to leaven the integrity of his translation. Ultimately, there should be no need whatever for him to remove himself from the rank and file of translators as such, or work in a special aura of privilege, in the name of "imitation." I say this without much hope that translators are ever any the wiser for having translated for a decade or a lifetime, or that they can ever hope for "Adam's dream," who "awoke and found it true." Indeed, Babel is always with us. The moralist will say, for example: Translation is a long discipline of self-denial, a matter of fidelity or betrayal: *traduttore, traditore.* The vitalist will say: Translation is a matter of life and death, merely: the life of the original or the death of it. The poet will say: Translation is either the composition of a new poem in the language of the translator, or the systematic liquidation of a masterpiece from the language of the original. The epistemologist will say: Translation is an illusion of the original forced upon the translator at every turn because he has begun by substituting his own language and occasion for that of the poet and must fabricate his reality as he goes. The Sibyl sees all and says: Translation is the truth of the original in the only language capable of rendering it "in truth": the original language untouched by translation.

3

Neruda's *Joaquín Murieta*:
A Note on the Poetics of Translation

I f, as Valéry supposed, poems are not completed but abandoned, it may be equally true of plays written in verse that their completion must be constantly re-invented. The play that is written with words must constantly alter its inflection and contend with both the contemporaneity of its audience and the waywardness of the theater as such. Audience and actor are engaged in a constant labor of revision. If the actor is to weep for Hecuba, the tears must be partly his own: he cannot be less than modern. And when the trap springs on the conscience of the king, the spectator must feel it in *his* bones rather than the playwright's or the actor's. Gertrude Stein once suggested that a play is always seen in two dimensions of time: Time Past, in which we savor and engage all that we have already experienced and enlist the total validation of our lifetime; and Time Present, in which we constantly experience a moment of unprecedented relatedness of the drama. Presumably, the joining of the two creates the "abstract and brief chronicle of the time" that theatre buffs have hoped for since *Hamlet*.

In this sense, all plays are in a constant state of "translation." The director "translates" the play into an equivalence of his own vision of its histrionic and philosophical force, brings it out of the courtyard or the folio, onto an apron, a wagon, a turn-table, a bare set of planks; throws a line of fire between the spectators and the players, or dissolves it with symbiotic encounters of the two; shows it in the round, or the three-

67

quarters, or minus a fourth wall, with plaster grapes and cupids climbing a proscenium as if to remind us of the mythological origin of our pleasure. The actor wears the play like a mask or his own skin: he "translates" the text by voicing and moving the word and investing it with the physical integrity of his function. The designer "translates" it by bounding the spaces and devising the ambience for an action. He can either deliver the play from representation with commanding hallucinations of his own, or show us Alice's looking-glass world with all its furniture still intact, but reading from right to left, rather than vice-versa, like a page of Hebrew: "stage-right," presumably, would be "holding a mirror up to nature."

What, then, is left for the translator to translate? Everything—and something in excess of all the moving and shaking for which enacted plays are destined. In the first place, it should be perfectly obvious that the translator is involved in a moving of languages—a monumental changing of the sounds, that permeates every function of *performance* and forces an imaginative engagement with all the exigencies which govern the mysteries of theatrical communication: the time of the play, both inside and out, the speed and passion of the actor's sensibility and the audience's involvement, the charismatic authority of the language, and that secret marriage of affinities which makes plays *playable* and touches the "occupation" of the player. In the second place, the translator re-invents the dynamics of the dramatic undertaking: its literal action in the Aristotelian sense of the word: the transmutation of energies into words which order the tension of a total enterprise and fix its somatic and symbolic immediacies: immediate character, immediate consequence, the immediate and shapely *doing* of all that needs to be done: the *dromenon*.

In the case of plays formalized as *poems*, the translator must reckon with yet another dimension which is the province of poetry itself: with the force that called words from the void and gave language to everything felt and envisioned in the play—the spiritual priority of poetry over every other consideration, in so far as the utterance itself is to be poetry. It is tempting, under the circumstances, to postulate the inherent equivalence of poetry and drama, but despite the long history of their coexistence, a better case can be made for the *antipoetic* character of theater. The record of poets who have deviated into drama—playable, voiceable drama—does not suggest that plays are the gratuitous outcome of poetry. Everything indicates that the poet is the first to fail at his drama and the last to blot out a line in the interests of the drama's effectiveness. Neruda himself, a self-confessed "apprentice," (*"aprendiz de teatrero"*) had the good humor to register his frustration in a kind of curtain speech* drafted from the safe distance of Isla Negra. There were, he says, "verses that rhymed as they did in my palmiest days . . . and dances, with music by Sergio Ortega, and Pedro Orthous, that famous theatrical director, to make his cut in the pie . . . urging this little change and that little deletion . . . and if I protested I was told the same thing had happened to Shakespeare and Lope de Vega . . . they snipped with their scissors and changed things around for your pleasure . . . after all, I am only a stagestruck apprentice . . . I gave in to everything so that Murieta could ride again."

And now there comes a translator like myself, resolved to translate the Spanish of a play—as though it were *still* a work-in-progress!—"for the American theater and the American voice": a permutation unforeseen even by Neruda. Very probably, the translators who preceded me in Italy, Germany, and France have already justified the playwright's determination never again to tempt the tragic muse in the collective bedlam of its original state—a region haunted by directors, producers, corporations, audiences, angels, electricians, by Spectacle and Action, masked dancers, musicians, designers, royalty on stilts and gods in machines. I should like only to make a case for the anomaly of my predicament as English translator; or more to the point, American translator.

Splendor and Death of Joaquín Murieta is a geographically American play. It joins two continents together by traveling northward from Valparaíso, crossing the Central American peninsula into Mexico, and planting itself on the Barbary Coast and the foothills of the Mother Lode, like a tropical liana, in a fantasy of hemispheric greed. Its scope is pan-American, but its locus is San Francisco, U.S.A., and the weight of its history is specifically *yanqui*. For Chileans, it is a play about disenfranchised compatriots in a country of rapists and capitalistic bigots. For North American readers—ourselves—it concerns Latin American aliens in an ambience to which we alone hold the linguistic and psychological keys. As "host-country," California makes unique demands on the plausibility of the language for readers in the United States, quite as much as any Californian's play about Anaconda Copper in Chile would be accountable to South Americans for the inflection and credibility of its participants. More than a substitution of one "rush" for another, of copper and nitrates

---

*Pablo Neruda, "¿Por qué Joaquín Murieta?", *Obras Completas* (Buenos Aires, Editorial Losada, 1968), II, pp. 1133-1134.

for gold, or United Fruit for Joaquín Murieta, is involved in the theatrical transaction. Playwright and translator alike must reckon with the American *sound* itself, as well as the sound of "poetry"—find an intonation which checks with whatever is idiosyncratic to the *yanqui* sense of history, his real or imagined vision of its archetypes: cowboys, 'forty-niners, vigilantes, pitchmen, desperados.

Of course, it is possible to dismiss such considerations as misguided and false to the spirit of what Neruda himself has quixotically called an opera, a pantomime, a melodrama, a jeu-d'esprit, a song, a tragedy and an "insurrectionary cantata." It is possible, that is to say, to read *Splendor and Death* non-representationally, from beginning to end, as a Hollywood "horse opera" enlisting the conventions of cinematic American mythology quite as much as it professes to adapt the conventions of Japanese Noh drama, with an equivalent suspension of disbelief in everything but the fact of theater itself. A histrionic rather than a historical stereotype of American violence, derived from Puccini, D. W. Griffith, and Hollywood westerns, will serve for Neruda's translators in Germany, Italy, and France, quite as much as they appear to have served for Neruda himself. *All* may be equally quaint: the "Hooded Figures" (*encapuchados*) enacting their barbaric rites of preemption and genocidal slaughter, the Beheaded Bandit, many times larger than life, speaking out of his cage in a Yokohaman funeral cortège, the choruses of Latin American keeners tuning their laments to the "high style" of neo-Grecian tragedy, the vaudeville turns of Box and Cox, or Laurel and Hardy, in the plain prose of John Threefingers and Reyes, the rapid-fire patter exchanged by the Gentleman Swindler and his Accomplices in the prosody of Gilbert and Sullivan and the style of the Spanish *zarzuela*.

For the *yanqui* reader, however, born to the feel of the "cowboy-and-Indian" myth, a further dimension of credulity is demanded. Audiences in this country have a right to expect an American "sound" not present in the inflection of Neruda, a sound native to the klansman and the conman, rather than to history, politics, or the ethics of vindication professed by the poet. The "heavies" of an American horse opera ought, at the very least, to display some of the expertise (admittedly a jargon!) of Caliban—a true artist in the theater, as Auden has shown us—who roundly berated his creator: "You taught me language and my profit on't / Is, I know how to curse." The bullies of Neruda do not know how to curse: they have not learned how to invite a quarrel or fan the passions of a lynch mob in the vernacular: not even in the vernacular of the Hollywood western. They are not sinister. Neruda is content merely to indicate, with an alien's English: "Shut up! Damn you! Go to hell!"; or "You are now in California. *Here's no chicha!* In California you must have whiskey!"—and doubtless his translators in Italy, France, and Germany will see nothing odd in all this.

These are linguistic considerations bearing on the *playableness* of the play, and as such, a concern of the translator who translates for the stage, rather than the closet or classroom. To this extent, I suppose, portions of Episodes Three and Four, incidental songs laced with Latin-American placenames and spinning their rhythms out of the pyrotechnical patter of the barker, occasional lyrics which must *sing* their way to an English end as they did in the Spanish, may be called "adaptations" of their originals. Occasionally, I have condensed a sequence of lines in the interests of "American" momentum—with, I trust, due regard for sense and continuity; and in one case I omitted a fanciful turn of action—the attempt of the klansmen to revive their "dead" Kleagle with a ritual dance—where the overload threatened to blow every fuse in the switchboard. Two café tunes written in English by Neruda and intended for a Black and a Blond Singer in Episode Three I have reserved for the Appendix, where they may be retrieved by both the historian and the producer who choose to restore them to their original sequence. It is no disservice to Neruda to say that his English and mine do not mix; but in every other respect I have worked for systematic fidelity to the context and spirit of the original Spanish: for a translation rather than an adapter's overlay.

The point needs to be made because Neruda himself in a prefatory note has urged extraordinary liberties upon his directors which might easily seduce the "creative" translator: the right to "invent situations and props to their liking" (*"para que invente situaciones u objetos fortuitos"*). My own intention, however faultily pursued, has been precisely the opposite: I have opted for the *poetry* of *Splendor and Death* in the belief that the play as poem, "cantata," song, is the deepest concern of Neruda and carries the total authority of his signature. Indeed, the poem *as poem* not only preceded the play, but is retained virtually intact, with a scant handful of omissions and its symmetry untouched, within the play itself, as a kind of progressive scenario. The classical quarrel between "epic poetry" and "tragic drama" as modes of truth in the transmutation of poetry into theater is not the concern of Neruda. In Neruda's poetics of tragedy the poem preceded the play by a year and was one of twelve "episodes" or "sea chanteys" incorporated in an ambitious sequence of *"barcarolas"** devoted to Rubén Darío, Rubén Azócar, Lord Cochrane of Chile, astronauts, Paris, Russia, and Latin American earthquakes, as a kind of nautical celebration of the poet's wife, Matilde Urrutia. One such *"barcarola"* which concludes Volume V of his *Memorial de Isla Negra* (1964) and was later transposed into *La barcarola* as an induction to his muse, was actually entitled "Amores: Matilde," as if to prefigure the love of Joaquín for the girl of Coihueco. In the laconic footnote to his play entitled "Why Joaquín Murieta?" Neruda reports, between suspension points:

> I wrote a big book of poems . . . I called it *The Barcarole* . . . a kind of ballad . . . I nibbled a bit of this and a bit of that out of my stock of poetic staples . . . and in this book there are episodes that sing and tell stories . . . that's how I do things . . . from the very beginning . . . can't manage otherwise . . . well . . . one day I picked and I prodded, a great cloud of dust arose like the tail end of an earthquake, flying around till it turned into an episode about a horse and its rider and started to gallop about in my verses—very long verses, this time, like highways or thoroughfares . . . and I rode herd behind them, verses and all, and struck gold, California gold with Chileans panning the sand and schooners under a full load of canvas sailing out of Valparaiso . . . then my wife, Matilde Urrutia, said: but isn't this theater, real theater? . . . and I answered, How should I know?

The initiating poem, like the play, bore the title of *Fulgor y muerte de Joaquín Murieta*, and the "very long verses"—the most sonorous and Gongoresque in the repertory of Neruda—recall the heroic hexameters, dactyllic and anapestic by turns, of Stesichorus of Himera, the great "choirsetter" from whom Pindar is supposed to have learned the grand style of choral oratory. They recur in the play without forfeiting so much as a karat's weight of their original pomp, with all their internal rhymes— often three to a line of verse—intact, ingeniously infiltrated into Male Choruses, Women's Choruses, quartets, trios, duets or orchestral dialogs in which stanzas are broken into antiphonal choruses for massed speakers and dancers, in Greek forensic style. Thus, the opening stanza of *La barcarola* also opens the play as a Prolog assigned to the Voice of the Poet; and the Voice of the Poet constantly recurs to remind us that Neruda's "insurrectionary cantata" is still, at its deepest level, the *drama of the making of a poem*. As in the original poem, the poet is constantly present in

---

*Neruda, "¿Por qué Joaquín Murieta?", *Obras Completas*, II, pp. 755-856.

his drama of *"Splendor and Death,"* meditating the occasion of his poem, appraising the morality of his hagiography of violence, vindicating the banditry of his hero, mediating, justifying, disclosing: the theophanic god-in-the-machine of his contrivance. By Episode Three, the poet, considering "the right and the wrong of this Bandit's Cantata" can say: "I call the rage of my countryman just." In the final episode, the Head of Murieta openly invokes the Poet-Behind-the-Play as his *deus ex machina*:

> What intruder
> or friend, tracing the naked truth
> in the snow,
> shall interpret my story or sing it
> in truth, in the end?
> My time is a hundred years hence.
> My lips shall be Pablo Neruda.

And at the play's end, it is the author of *La barcarola* himself who steps out, in plain view of the audience, hexameters and hendecasyllables still unscathed, to pronounce the poet's epilogue, precisely as it was in the sea-song:

> You were one of your country's Romantics;
> not mine to censure the outcome: a
> cavalcade fearful and fiery;
> or construe its destruction. I saw only
> a brave man went under.
> For spirits like yours, no path leads
> back to an option. They blunder,
> their teeth grating fire, they burn,
> they rise like a phoenix,
> then return to their faraway eyrie.
> They take life from the coals that
> consume them; the coal
> burns them back to a cinder.

> Joaquín, return to your nest: gallop the air
> toward the South on your blood-colored stallion.
> The streams of the country that bore you
> sing out of silvery mouths.
> Your Poet sings with them.

III

Prefaces to Translation:

Practice

*What is the thing that translators
can know, and how can their
language know it?*

4

Translator's Preface:
Four Poems by Rimbaud

A word of explanation is due the reader with regard to the procedure followed here. In departing from recent practice of printing the English translation and the French texts on opposite leaves, I have been guided by two considerations. In the first place, I have sought to anticipate the misuse of the texts by readers who, in effect, presuppose the existence of an imaginary paradigm, and preside over the translator's function like umpires in a tennis match, on the assumption that French and English must be played to a dead heat. In the second place, I have sought to avoid the positivism of those translators who approach the poem as coin of the realm, to be manipulated by the expedient of converting French counters into English, like francs into dollars.

Certainly, the first duty of reader and translator is to the French original, where deviations of language and syntax can be identified as such and the translator's responsibilities measured accordingly. With this in mind, I have supplied literal renderings of all French texts in an appendix in which attention is directed solely upon the information of the original *as information*, and the poem is made available to the reader as a document. The *translations*, on the other hand, are distinguished from the literal renderings by a difference of function. Here the attempt has been to communicate poetry *as poems*, to be read in their right as English poems, with the form and afflatus of the original translated not intact, but as the character of the language has demanded their eventuation in English.

It is a curious fact that, in an epoch of methodologies, the semantics of translation has so far gone unexamined.* It is, however, one thing to

---

*The naiveté of this remark and the bounty available to students and practitioners today will be apparent at once from George Steiner's recent prolegomenon to translation in our time, *After Babel*, concede with poets and critics generally that Rimbaud is an "untranslatable" poet, and another to proceed, as translators must, on the assumption that such statements are _actually_ true. In the present versions, I have accepted the untranslatability of Rimbaud as a tool of procedure and a measure of the task to be accomplished. I believe in all conscience that I have undertaken an impossible transaction, and that the translator's task must be accomplished _within_ the untranslatable factor itself. To this end I have sought to achieve "accuracy" within the spirit of the poetic process, and at times against the grain of the translated word, in the hope of recovering a poem. I have sought, in other words, to translate _relationships_, instead of single words, and have erred consistently on the side of temerity.

---

and the selective bibiliography (1813-1973) from which he enlists his erudition. The accomplishment is awesome in the refinement and sophistication of its inquiry into "those aspects of language and translation" which have engaged the thinking of exegetes from Cicero and Saint Jerome to Walter Benjamin and Cline, and in the rigor of its deliberations. If a prospectus for a "school of translators" such as those which are said to have existed in Bagdad and Alexandria between 100 and 800 A.D. were wanting, Professor Steiner's summation is as good as a college quadrivium. The gamut of oppositions —spirit and letter, meaning and sense, deep structures and surface grammars, object and word, "monadism" and universalism, linearity and field, semiotic and idiolectic meaning—and the abundance of its choices, may require another decade for assimilation by translators still to come. I share Professor Steiner's surmise that "there is no privileged access to the underlying totality" of translation, and that because of "the very nature of language and linguistic diversity, they are inseparable from the functions of non-information, privacy, and poetics which are the creative attributes of human speech." "Imagination" is my word—not Professor Steiner's—for this semantics of "radical indeterminacy."   —B.B.

Translator's Preface:
Poet in New York

No apology, I hope, is needed for the new translation of a work which refers its author most directly to the American reader. It was to American readers in the broadest sense of the term—the South American readers of Neruda's *Canto general de Chile* and the Mexican readers of Martinez' *Los senderos ocultos*, as well as to the "vomiting multitudes" of Coney Island and the somnambulists of Brooklyn Bridge—that the poem was initially addressed by its publishers in Mexico, Argentina, and New York, a decade after its completion in Havana and four years after the inexpiable murder of the poet. Today, *Poet in New York* remains an indispensable book for readers of two Americas.

This translator, along with a generation of American readers, is initially in debt to the example of Rolfe Humphries' pioneering version of *Poet in New York*, and to the passion that held him to his task at a time when no fair or definitive text could be found by his publishers in this country. The claim of translators today must be a modest one, by comparison: that of augmenting a provisional and defective text with a full and authoritative one, emending deviant or faulty readings, repairing omissions of punctuation and errors of typography, and limiting the hazards of a poem already famous for its "obscurity" to those which are irreducibly a part of the poet's intention.

To these objectives, I have added another which may furnish the true occasion for the present translation. My concern, in a very real sense, has been a double one: that of exploring a *dimension* of translation, as well as an artifact of contemporary Spanish culture. No translator can long expose himself to the harassing fire of two linguistic happenings—that which is given to him by a poem originally conceived within the contexts of a language not his own, as a completed action; and that which he seeks to create for it out of the resources of his own tongue—and remain incurious of his function.

It has not been my assumption, as it was Mr. Humphries', that these poems "cannot, and should not, be expected to sound . . . like English poems, or American ones." That the "effects of Spanish verse are not ours," and that the English equivalences can never be identical with the Spanish, is both a truism inherent in the modality of language and an enigma inexhaustible to thought. The day when "the whole earth was of one language" is not yet returned, and the generations of Babel continue to plague the translator. His premise, at the outset, must be a hard one: that the *poem* in English will not follow gratuitously upon the poem in Spanish, once the English *word* has followed "accurately" upon the Spanish; that their textures and durations will differ, word by word, and word after word, and that the differences will deepen and compound with unimaginable complexity with the collocations of words; that syntax distributes and assembles identical notions with differing tensions in differing languages; that words, in whatever language, have a history which is not Esperanto or Sanskrit, or the "history of mankind," but the cultural consequence of their activity in the linguistic experience of a group—for chauvinism is an inalienable property of all language; that words must be ascended and descended, like buckets in a well, rather than joined in a series like pipe-lengths; and finally, that for the poet, the momentum of words is as important and mysterious a trust as their matter, and that their momentum—their *brio*, their capacity to reveal the spirit at work within the letter—is rooted irrationally in the densities and ambiguities of the individual language.

Nonetheless, it would be my conviction that a translator who is content with *translating out of* one language only, has completed only one half the transaction, and that the harder task of *translating into* his own remains to be confronted. It is a task, needless to say, full of risk and uncertainty—in the lonely sign of translation where the translator, forever on the *other* side of his original, reconceives the solitude of the creator on *his* side of the binder's seam, and, like the imagining man of Coleridge, "dissolves, dissipates, diffuses," in order to create anew. It is here that the true "morality" of translation may be said to reside, its real conscience: in an exploration of real temptations, real perils, real equivalences, from which the trot and the hack and the self-serving complacencies of the "accurate" way are excluded. Here, in short, the translator is at liberty to contemplate the universe of the given poem as its creator originally contemplated the universe of his given experience—not as a datum substantively present in the nature of things, but as a precarious search for exactitudes, correspondences, analogies which will mirror their model only in flashes, and which will demonstrate nothing so much as its partial knowability in the end.

I am in debt to José F. Montesinos for reading together with me in the Spanish each of the essays and certain of the poems included in this volume; for his illumination of ambiguities and nuances insoluble to myself; for the providential correction of error, and direct insights into the mind and sensibility of the poet which have at times made conjecture seem like a species of inspiration. To Dr. Montesinos—and equally to Dr. Angel del Río of Columbia University—I owe the additional kindness of a close review of the final manuscript—doubtless less punishing than should be—which has often helped me temper the afflatus of the English to a reading more in keeping with the original, and reconsider the alternatives available to me. I am grateful to the poet's brother, Francisco García Lorca, for his assistance in fixing the Spanish text—which in the main accords with the model of the 1940 Mexican edition—and for additional help in construing images and allusions whose contexts steadfastly eluded me. It would be a disservice to these and other benefactions to imply that the present version fairly reflects the authority of either their intimate acquaintance with the poet or their deeper comprehension of the tradition of Spanish poetry. Nevertheless, I have sought, in all conscience, to measure my choices in the light of their considered responses, and to employ the added resonance as a clue to the fidelity or impertinence of my own efforts.

A word with regard to the Critical Chronology and the Appendices of essays, poems, and fugitive prose pieces which complete the design of this volume. The Chronology, I am bound to confess, is a counsel of desperation arising from the need to encompass a complex and extenuated textual history whose recital in any other form would have numbed the reader. It is my hope that the facts, in their present guise, combine the *longueurs* of bibliography with the spice of amateur detection, and deliver intact the story of a manuscript's total emergence. The aims of the Appendices are several: principally, to impound "missing" or conjectural poems which fall into the orbit of *Poet in New York*, but whose order in the canon cannot be established for reasons made known in the Chronology; to document the Chronology by every means available to the translator and inaccessible to the general reader; and to suggest the development of Lorca's "surrealist" manner from his earliest exercises in "style" to the visceral agonies of his vision of the City.

Two essays, little known in this country, have also been included in the Appendices, in the belief that *Poet in New York* raises esthetic and compositional problems as dismaying to readers of Lorca's popular *romances* as his tormented use of the New York scene; and that, for such readers, these essays, between jest and earnest, will measure the sources of the poet's imaginative commitment. The essay on Góngora, which William Carlos Williams has commended to all practitioners of poetry "to read and have to heart," is reproduced in a slightly abbreviated version; the essay on the *Duende*, with the exception of certain opening amenities, is translated in full for the first time.

The rewards of these essays, as the reader will readily discover, are considerable, and would require a Foreword beyond the scope of these pages to suggest. Particularly significant, however, is the ambivalence of Lorca's case for both the willed and the mantic in art—for the "inspired state" from which "one returns as from a foreign country," and for the ritual exercise of techniques applied by the poet to their last refinement of intended effectiveness. The "surrealism" of *Poet in New York* involves, obviously, a suspension of those controls: a journey into the adventitious and the nocturnal like that of his Hunter in the forest of the "thousand splendors and the thousand hideous masks of the splendid," or the baroque improvisations of Pastora Pavon, the "Girl With the Combs." It culminates in a literature of the *grito*: the *cry*, which has little in common with the Gallic importations of Rafael Alberti or his models in Apollinaire and Breton. Its sources, as his remarkable entertainment on the *Duende* will make clear, are no less regional and Hispanic than the ballads of Lorca's popular manner. Unlike those ballads, however, *Poet in New York* probes *behind* the flamenco invention—behind the impacted spontaneities of the *saeta, siguiriya, petenera, soleá*—to the frenzy, the shudder, the paroxysm, the "deep song" and the "dark root of the cry" out of which they emerge. It moves directly into the savagery of the psychic occasion, to enact an agon of self-knowledge, unmediated by form, in an imagery of blood, spittle, excrement, alcohol, nausea, madness, and cathartic dance.

For if the Gypsy ballads were a tribal and formalized manifestation of the *gitanismo* of García Lorca, the *Poet in New York* is a private improvisation on its sensibility. With good reason Alfredo de la Guardia, in the course of his appraisal of the poem, pauses to ask with unfeigned incredulity:

> *"Ay, Harlem!*
> *Ay, Wall Street!"*

> What is the meaning of that *Ay!*—the mark of flamenco lament, the wail of the "deep song"—in a Stock Exchange world that, in the course of that very year (1929), was to scatter the dynamite charge of its stocks and certificates to all sides and explode in a prodigious crash?

For somewhere between the parable of the Hunter, and the "black sounds" (*"sonidos negros"*) of Pastora Pavon, lie the landscapes of Lorca's New York, in the keeping of that daimon who "smashes the styles" and paints with its "fists and its knees in bituminous blacks," and announces "the unending baptism of all newly-created things."

6

Translator's Preface:
Juan de Mairena

Tradition has reserved this space for the translator's apology for his translation. Machadians will not have to be informed of the hazards of translating either the prose of *Juan de Mairena* or the lyrics of the *Apocryphal Songbooks*; and apology is probably lost upon those who assume that Machado, a master of the "middle style," and a conspicuous adversary of the baroque, is *always* leathery, open, and linear, "like the landscapes of Castile." A. Sańchez Barbudo, in his tour de force of clarification, *The Thought of Antonio Machado*, takes pains to remind the casual reader of the "enigmatic" and "disconcerting" character of the *Apocryphal Songbooks* and the "obscurity of the philosophical writings." Similarly, the author of *The World and the Work of Antonio Machado** is concerned with the "mirror play," the "screens," the "apocryphal compensations," and the "hermetic" aspects of the later Machado. All present problems for the translator which may well prove insuperable.

In another sense, however, it has always been the translator's task to devise an "apocryphal life" for a text which can have no second being apart from the linguistic and imaginative processes intrinsic to its original containment of experience. "The only living language," Mairena somewhere remarks, "is the language in which we think and have our being. We are given only one . . . we must content ourselves with the surfaces, grammatical and literary, of all the others." The "Otherness" with which Mairena/Martín/Machado are all severally preoccupied and which the translator presumably shares—which "persists and suffices for itself" and

---

*Segundo Serrano Poncela, *Antonio Machado: Su mundo y su obra* (Buenos Aires: Editorial Losado, S.A., 1954).

"will submit to no elimination"—has its absolute in the work of art from which translation begins. Here, it would seem, art has achieved what logic and contemplation—least of all, translation!—could not: the unique engagement of language and sensibility in an artifact which, once realized, remains "immutable, anchored forever, as it were, in the river of Heraclitus"; for which the only mode of existence is the mode of its original being.

However, as Machado also reminds us, "we live in an essentially apocryphal world, a cosmos or poem of our thinking, ordered and structured on undemonstrable suppositions"; and it is here that the translator may find both the premise of his vocation and the necessary autonomy of his commitment. In *Juan de Mairena*, where the spectrum of "Otherness" is already multiple, and the "screens," masks, doubles, and transpositions threaten the world of the poet with that Nothingness which Martín preëmpted for his God, the translator has a special labor of fidelity. He must play "Class Listener," like Mairena's "*oyente*," to the many voices of Machado as they have already shaped the intonation of his prose style: the magisterial mode of the schoolteacher, smelling faintly of chalk and the morning *tertulia*; the sententious and hortatory inflection of the moralist, with its blend of intimacy and asperity; the colloquial turns which are there because the speaker, a man of gregarious habits, has declared for a literature that is "spoken" rather than "written"; the poet concerned with enigma, and the philosopher concerned with ideality, turning bafflement into irony and misgivings into aphorisms. These are rhetorical specifics for the literature of a wry and hermetic intelligence; these are linguistic particulars for that "heterogeneity of Being" which the poet enacts and the translator simulates.

The Appendix of poems from the *Apocryphal Songbooks* (in a sequence which is mine, not Machado's) are another matter, differing in the mode of their translation as the exigencies of poetry differ from prose. Here the attempt has been to communicate the power and density of the originals by equivalent facts of *form*, in a matrix of English which at times transposes the Spanish effects directly, and at other times builds on the thrust of English prosody, as a collateral "fact of form." The hope is to suggest by this means the *internality* of Machado's lyricism—its hermetic integrity, if you wish; not, however, in the manner of the hermit crab who backs himself into the shell of larger crustaceans, but by parallel acts of self-containment. Thus, much of "The Death of Abel Martín" reproduces a line-for-line profile of the original, with incidental transpositions of content and prosody; and the English of "Two Songs" might be said literally to follow *after* the Spanish of Antonio Machado, to achieve a monolithic entirety of song by processes inherent to English. Here, emendation and paraphrase are more frequent, especially in the "untranslatable" locutions of a syntax which is fluid in Spanish and polyglot in English; but in each instance I have sought to render the pulls of meaning and melody organically comparable.

As editor, I also have to account for the diminished equivalence of a text which, in its original version, runs to 324 pages, as published by Espasa-Calpe in Madrid in 1936. One hopes, of course, for a distillation and not a mutilation of the essential Machado, preserving the total balance of his preoccupations as apocryphal Juan—the poetics, metaphysics, politics (in the conceptual sense), pedagogy, dialectic, rhetoric, theology, and *belles-lettres*; the passion for *otredad* ("Otherness"), *la nada* ("Nothingness"—and a Spaniard's Nothingness is like nobody else's), *heterogeneidad* ("heterogeneity"), *el Ser* ("Being"); and assorted ironical entertainments. I have omitted all later emendations, pendants, and appendices, largely patriotic and political, of the "posthumous" Mairena, which follow the 1936 canon, and the extended poetics attached to the *cancioneros* of Martín and Mairena, which should some day be translated intact. The complexity and sweep of the latter, as Barbudo has ably demonstrated, are indisputable; but for that very reason, their intrusion in the present volume would tilt the balance of masks, identities, screens, and impersonations, and misplace the gravity of that apocryphal world which, in *Juan de Mairena*, is not encompassed but suspended. The result, I am satisfied, is a treasury of the mind and sensibility of a major imaginative intelligence, cut to the sequences and the fifty chapters of the original and preserving their total ensemble.

In the guise of poet, immersed in the labor of translating and construing a creative phenomenon and viewing it from the stance of ontological criticism, I should like to venture an afterthought. Recent scholarship has focused sedulously on the philosophical texture of Machado's accomplishment, and for very good reason. It *is* substantively philosophical in both its effects and its sources, and its ambiguities require the glosses of the historian of ideas. That a philosopher-poet who aims at "maximizing temporality" should himself be volatilized in time in the end—in depth as well as in historical extension—is by no means surprising; and with

Machado, there is reason to probe for conceptual and metaphysical consequences. The area has been abundantly delved by Barbudo, Poncela,
Aranguren, Bellé, de Torre, and others, and the affinities with Heidegger,
Bergson, Jaspers, Unamuno, the early phenomenologists and the later
existentialists, are available to connoisseurs of letters and ideas.

It may be time again to view the identical circumstance "poetically,"
as Machado himself preferred to view both the meanings and the modality
of philosophy—from Kant's dove and Heraclitus' river (and Archimedes'
lever?) to the culminating refinements of Heideggerian *"Sorge."* Seen from
this vantage point, it is the *apocryphal*, rather than the "existential,"
datum which becomes primary: all the modes of simulation and dissimu-
lation by which a poet accommodates himself to his own strangeness and
displaces the world with his being. Put it another way: the daimon of the
Apocrypha points to Creation, and the angel of Existenz points to Being
—both, in the spirit of Mairena's benevolent diabolism: "You have excel-
lent parents who deserve your respect and affection: why not go on to
invent better?"

So viewed—as invention rather than meditation—it is Kierkegaard,
rather than Heidegger or Bergson, who emerges as the apocryphal double
or "familiar" of Antonio Machado. The affinities, I dare say, are analogical
rather than demonstrable—a kinship of identities, rather than a collation
of conceptual thought. Yet they are there, just as the invention present in
the minds of two discrete intelligences, saturated with the immanence of
things to come but widely separated in space, might simultaneously
produce the incandescent bulb or the second law of thermodynamics.
There comes to mind, first of all, the fact of their mutual compulsion for
the pseudonymous life—in the sense that Poncela insists it should apply
here: Machado-Mairena-Martín, on the one hand, and Kierkegaard on the
other in the guise of the Seducer, or the Editor presiding over the
simulated identities of the "A" of *Either* and the "B" of *Or*, and signing
himself "Victor Eremita" (as in "hermetic"). Like Machado, the editorial
Eremita is preoccupied with a tactic of doubleness and systematic hoax,
and its confessional revelations of being: "In the confessional, the priest is
separated from the penitent by a screen; he does not see, he only hears.
Gradually, as he listens, he constructs an outward appearance which cor-
responds to the voice he hears. Consequently, he experiences no contradic-
tion. It is otherwise, however, when you hear and see at the same time
and yet perceive a screen between yourself and the speaker." Like Ma-

chado, too, Kierkegaard, caught in the anguish of the apocryphal life, is compelled to concede at last: "One author seems to be enclosed in another, like the parts of a Chinese puzzle-box . . . The dominant mood of A's preface in a manner betrays the poet. It seems as if A had actually become afraid of his poem, as if it continued to terrify him, like a troubled dream when it is told."

It is precisely at this point that the nuances begin to multiply. If Machado has his brandy bottle and his greatcoat to fortify the inner and outer man of his "professor" and cloak the "memoranda, epigrams, maxims, *et cetera*" of a philosopher *manqué*, Kierkegaard had his apocryphal escritoire, purchased at second hand and honeycombed with secret recesses, which, at a lucky hatchet blow, spills out the manuscript pages of *Either/Or*. Nor is it surprising that, in one instance, the final stroke of the hatchet breaks open the box of the erotic, to reveal the "Diary of a Seducer"; and, in the second instance, that Machado focuses on Don Juan, in all his mutations, as "hero of the Christian temper," on the clothed and unclothed Maja, Jack the Ripper as a travesty of deprived paternity, a tragicomedy by Mairena called *The Grand Climacteric*, the randy diabolism of Espronceda, and a schoolboy's parody of dialectic on the theme of "Nudity and Liberty, Properly Understood."

The relation of the erotic to the apocryphal life in each instance is somber and teasing, and merits its fair share of illumination, along with Machado's affinities with the existentialists, as modes of being and compensation. Kierkegaard's broken engagement to Regina and the elegiac pathos of Machado as lifelong mourner, widower, and solitary are equally germane to the poetry of deprival and the philosophy of "ontological anguish." Certainly the theme of anguish—specifically, poetic anguish— is constant throughout the *Diapsalmata ad se ipsum* of Kierkegaard: "A critic resembles a poet to a hair, he only lacks the anguish of poets and the music on his lips. I tell you, I would rather be a swineherd understood by the swine, than a poet misunderstood by men." And the *lacrimae rerum* of Machado are similarly present in Kierkegaard, with an identical hermetic inflection: "I say of my sorrow what the Englishman says of his house: My sorrow is my castle." So, too, are the satanism of Don Juan and the Donjuanesque; the primacy of the folkloric; "the courage to doubt everything"; the faith in the clairvoyance of children and the indelible persistence of their memory; the themes of dread, futurity, and the mystery of identity

("One ought to be a mystery not only to others, but also to oneself."); the incompatibility of causes and effects, questions and answers; the preoccupation with Shakespeare, God, the classics, the Old Testament; apocalyptical presentiments of earthquake, waterspouts, judgment, death, and non-Being. Indeed, the shared preoccupations of Kierkegaard and Machado are circumstantial enough to constitute a "doubleness" which is no longer the invention of a conspiratorial intelligence, but a clue to our contemporaneity and that "essentially apocryphal" character of the world which, in Machado's view, produced the "cosmos or poem of our thinking."

In that "poem," Machado does not stand alone among his countrymen: the effect of his premise is rather to turn the whole literature of Europe into a parable of avid apocryphal quest. In the vanguard—or so Machado would have us believe—comes his beloved Cervantes in the guise of Quixote-Sancho Panza: a "twinned series of figures, real and hallucinatory . . . two integral, complementary consciousnesses, conversing and forging ahead." And moving into our own century, there follows an array of animal and human *Doppelgänger* whose passion for Otherness, heterogeneity, and the apocryphal has left its abiding mark on the literature of our epoch. Federico García Lorca readily comes to mind, in the masks of Camborio, Sanchez Mejías, *gitano legítimo*, a quartet of saints and a repertory of plays, with his child's outcry: "¡Qué raro que me llame Federico!" ("How odd to be called Federico!"); then Valle-Inclán, in the ruff and derring-do of Marques de Bradomín, "el mas admirable de los Don Juanes: feo, católico, y sentimental" ("the most admirable of the Don Juans: ugly, Catholic, and sentimental"), pursuing his doubleness in its erotic and seasonal guises; Rimbaud as *Vierge Folle* and *L'Époux Infernal* peering full face from a profile of Verlaine, like a portrait by Picasso, and calling to his counterfeits: "Duval, Dufour, Armand, Maurice, que sais-je? . . . A chaque être plusières autres vies me semblaient dues" ("Duval, Dufour, Armand, Maurice, how should I know? To each, I thought, many other lives had been given."); Rilke as Cornet Christopher, Knight of the Bilderbuch, and "other self" of Malte Laurids Brigge: "Sie werden sich hundert neue Namen geben und einander alle wieder abnehmen, leise, wie man einen Ohrring abnimmt." ("They will give each other a hundred new names and take them away as lightly as one takes off an earring."); Mallarmé as des Esseintes: "Nous fûmes deux, je le mantiens!" ("I insist, we were two!"); Eliot as J. Alfred Prufrock: "No, I am not

Prince Hamlet, nor was meant to be / Am an attendant lord . . . "); Yeats in the hermetic panoply of the Mask and the Image, stalking the daimon of his Anti-Self on the Path of the Chameleon:

> I, that my native scenery might find imaginary inhabitants, half-planned a new method and a new culture. My mind began drifting vaguely toward that doctrine of "the mask" which has convinced me that every passionate man . . . is, as it were, linked to another age, historical or imaginary, where alone he finds images that rouse his energy . . . Image called up image in an endless procession, and I could not always choose among them with any confidence; and when I did choose, the image lost its intensity, or changed into some other image . . . I was lost in that region a cabalistic manuscript . . . had warned me of; astray upon the Path of the Chameleon, upon *Hodos Chameleontos*.

Thus, between Greek and Irish, Yeats, too, evokes the *Nada* of Machado and suggests its anguish.

Last of all, on his own soil, I would summon Juan Ramón Jiménez in the guise of the celebrated donkey of Moguer. Smelling deceptively of sweet marjoram and eating pomegranate kernels, he is actually a cosmology, like the tortoises of China or the Leviathan of the Hebrews, charged with the ambiguity of a myth and the immediacy of a totem animal. Summoned into being with all the tender variations of his name—Platero! Plateron! Platerillo! Platerete!—he takes shape in a pastoral haze, in a landscape where even the "flowering ground appears dreamlike, a strange lace, primitive, beautiful," drinking the sugary flesh of watermelons, at once vegetal and incarnate, fabulous and actual, secular and paschal, lyrical and irreducible. At his side, *within* him as well as *upon* him, goes the image of a poet not unlike Machado in temperament, "dressed in mourning, with my beard cut like a Nazarene's and my narrow-brimmed hat," among festivals and fast days, like a genius of uncommitted pathos. These, then, are the "apocrypha" of a century which has in every decade sent its poets back to the *Nada*, as Mairena sends the student to the blackboard, to trace on the void, in erasable chalk, improvisations of assertion and selfhood, in a timeless comedy of transcendence.

7

Translator's Preface:
The Selected Poems of Rafael Alberti

I f a "selected Alberti" implies an obligation to embrace the whole accomplishment of a poet, choose at will among the pieces assembled, and find the wit and the English to translate accordingly, this is not a "selected poems" of Rafael Alberti. I cannot pretend, for example, that I have chosen to exclude from this anthology that small sunburst of graces which makes the earliest volume of Alberti, *Marinero en tierra* (1925) and the volumes which follow it in 1925 (*La amante*) and 1927 (*El alba del alhelí*) so irresistible. The *coplas*, *madrigales*, and *pregones* go by default, rather than by choice: after years of trying to turn them into *faits* of translation, I have had to conclude, a little sullenly, they are paradisal soufflés whose chemical nature it was to rise only once. As Ricardo Gullon[1] has pointed out, "they appear to be pure emanations, transcending all effort"; they hover like spray on the wave of that childhood when, in Alberti's words, "my eyes were giddy with quicklime, packed with white salt from the estuaries, pierced by the blues and pure yellows, the violets and greens of my river, my ocean, my beaches, and pines."

For all their disarming immediacy, however—the effect of which is to suspend meditation and enchant with facts of pure pleasure—a touch of English reveals them to be artifacts of the poet's vocation, complex systems of rhythm, vagary, and refrain set into place with implacable virtuosity. One discovers, in an apparently airy "confection" from the *Marinero*, that all is irreducibly *substantive*, wrought into the time and the temper of the Andalusian "sound" as the wreath is wrought into the steel in the damascene art of Toledo. Rhythm for rhythm and word after word, they accomplish continuing miracles of utterance innate to the syntax and brio of the Spanish. The word falls where it wills, infallible, unforced, providential; and behind it, the whole balladic tradition of Spain is at work in its combination of the artful and the popular, investing the song of Alberti with pressures that pull at the depths of a language—specifically, the Spanish language—like the pull of a tide. They are intransmissible.

My defection is not helped by the fact that *Marinero en tierra* won for the poet of twenty-two the Premio Nacional de Literatura (1925), the nod of Antonio Machado and Menéndez Pidal, among other judges, and the thorny cordiality of Juan Ramón Jiménez, whose sponsoring letter introduces the poems with a seignorial expectation of fealty to come. Having confessed the partial failure of an intention, however, I should like to point out that, in all other respects, I believe this representation from the *Poesías completas* to be an actively "selective" one: some fifty poems from eleven volumes written over an interval of thirty years, with the emphasis bearing strongly on *Sobre los ángeles*, *Verte y no verte*, *A la pintura*, and the *Retornos de lo vivo lejano*—the gamut of Alberti as Gongorist, agonist, elegist, "poet in the street," painter, and exile.

The result, to be sure, is an Alberti *en tierra*, a land-locked Alberti: and an Alberti *en tierra* is primarily a poet of exile, a "lost Andalusian" whose dominant themes are bereavement, banishment, and nostalgia: *"arboledas perdidas"* (vanished groves), *"paraísos perdidos"* (lost paradises), *"retornos"* (returns), *"sombras malditas"* (accursed shadows), *"toros de la muerte"* (bulls of death) and similar phantasms of expatriation. His orbit is purgatorial rather than paradisal: a limbo presided over by an inchoate pantheon of angels, tubercular nightmares, neurasthenia, civil war, Keystone comedians, the mystique of the bullring and the demigods of the Prado, and the muse of intimate memory.

Doubtless, for the reader of Alberti accustomed to the indigo-and-aquamarine world of his "land-sailor," the picture demands a sobering reversal of perspective. C. M. Bowra[2] was among the first to emphasize the primacy of a "crisis of an imaginative spirit" concerned with "dark movements and situations of the soul," and to weigh the angelism of Alberti against the bicarbonated jubilation of his seascapes, his sailor blouses, Andalusian whitewashes, and that gift of balladic timing for which there is no word but *gracia*. As early as 1937, moreover, Dudley Fitts, whose eye for the depths and surfaces of literatures, past and present, provincial and exotic, is virtually infallible, introduced his *Poems (1929-1936)*[3] with a mordant epigraph from Alberti ("*Para ir al infierno, no hace falta cambiar de sitio ni postura*: To go to hell, one need never change place or position"). Fitts chose as title poem to his collection his "Homage to Rafael Alberti":

> Rafael, in your Cádiz, white against blue quadrate
> In your District of Angels, Cádiz,
> If there is cadence of wind or sun, bells
> Toll it, record it; and you
> Translate the liquid characters as they run
> The shudder of rain on the roofs is rain only,
> Rain, rain only; but within the rain your Angels—
> Informing rain and roofs and the stippled entries,
> The wine-shop cats crouched in the sweet dust of wine,
> Shell, wire, langosta, razorblade, musty files—
> Move hugely, quiet; and your stricken eyes
> Mark the santoral-sinew pulsing there,
> Throbbing,
> > Angel-rain, Angel-world, meaning-of-Angels,
> > Ladder of Cádiz, hallow-of-Angels-latent,
> The delicate armies, inward fire white
> Alleluyas of glass and bell, forever bright.

The selection of this anthology is weighted in the spirit of that mood. Between the angels and sailors of Albert's youth, and the melancholia of later works like the *Retornos de lo vivo lejano* (1952) and *Baladas y canciones del Paraná* (1953-1954), lies a lifetime of displacement and homesickness elegized in prose, in nostalgic detail, in an intimate *recherche du temps perdu*,[4] (*La arboleda perdida / A Vanished Grove*) complete to the Proustian adjective: *perdu*. Here, the lost, the banished, the repudiated—"*lo perdido*," "*lo lejano*"—emerge as obsessional themes of a postwar Alberti, just as the increasing formalization of his prosody reflects the pressures of exile and longing that drive "a rainy evening," "a birthday," "an abandoned museum," Chopin, and "love in a theater loge" through fastidious spirals of syntax and bereavement, like the humming in a shell. The reader in quest of the "complete" Alberti can never forget that, for all his earlier scintillation, the "quicklime and song" of his baroque and flamenco phases, his dominant signature is elegiac and his vocation, mourning.

It is my hope that these selections, with the accompanying excerpts from *A Vanished Grove*, will reflect the refinement and persistence of that motif, which is a "persistence of memory" not as di Chirico or Dalí, the friend of his youth, imagined it, magically distorted by mannequins, optical illusions, and the special lighting that turns even pebbles monstrous, but exactly as last encountered by the poet. In that world of total recall (*retornos*), all has been stopped as in a fairy story: "the delectable book fallen limp on the floor," the "currants and strawberries" in their "hidden recess," García Lorca in the "glaze of expensive alpaca as though recently turned by the shears," the "drench of immediate blues, wet blue over blues," "tablecloths on a table," the "abrupt or the gradual / running of wines," "pieces and clutter—Heaven knows what they mean." All is remembered with a grieving insistence upon family, *tierra*, and a long anguish of exile that, at its best, calls to mind the *Poemas humanos* of another casualty of expatriation, César Vallejo.

As to the mode of my translation, I have the customary misgivings and satisfactions, plus the edgy knowledge that in my search for equivalent outcomes, I have often been forced further from the literal than I would wish to go, *kept* there by the pulse I have placed under my English to give it character and "closure," and left with only a wet forefinger to measure which way the winds of equivalence were blowing. It was my conviction, for example, that the sonnets and tercets of Alberti, in which, as in Góngora, all is "resilient, transparent, and colorless," stored "in cut-crystal, in caskets and urns," must be confronted as such, rather than reduced to denotative puddings or lumps of invertebrate English. What to do, moreover, with a "flat" line from "*Carta abierta*":

Roma y Cártago frente a frente iban

literally rendered, "Rome and Carthage went face to face" (if not, indeed, forehead to forehead), but actually intending the work teams into which classrooms were competitively divided in provincial Jesuit schools, "Romans and Carthaginians," much as Joyce invoked them in his *Portrait* as "Lancaster and York"? Or the "castillos"

del Pím-Pám-Púm de los tres Reyes Magos

in the "*Guía estival del paraíso*," literally and inscrutably the "castles of Pim-Pam-Pum of the Three Magi," but intending a child's shooting gallery (Pím-Pám-Púm) where rubber balls serve in place of bullets or pellets, recalled in an overlay of Christmas festivity? Or the climactic groan of the elegist in *Verte y no verte*:

Había olvidado ahora que la hablaba de usted no de tú, desde siempre

literally "I had forgotten now I have been speaking to you as *usted* [formal address] not as *tú* [intimate address] all along." Or the unabashed churrigueresqueries of "*El niño de la Palma*," "*Goya*," or "*Gutierrez Solana*":

> *Lo mas pálido*
> *ético*
> *perlético*
> *perlipelambrético . . .*
> *lo mas goyesco*
> *quevedesco*
> *valle-inclanesco*
> *del cuesco*

Indeed, there is good reason to question whether any language that issues from the art and the hammer of the poem can be neutrally approached or remain "literal." The fact of placement, of long marination in the tension and time of the poet's experience, the vatic thrust that commits it from the unforeseeable, to the shaping *poiesis* that sustains and astonishes the poet in the end, preempt "literal" outcomes. Precisely to the extent that a poem is never *foresayable*, and that paraphrase, criticism, and elucidation remove themselves from the afflatus that imagined the parts, and deal only with the *said*, it repels "literal" reduction. Even the notion that a poem, once composed, is a *terminal* datum is an imaginative rather than a literal one; nor do we need Valéry to remind us that poems are not terminated but abandoned.

Semantically, the "terminal fallacy" leads to the further illusion that the *words* in the poem are terminal, as words in a dictionary are thought to be so, and must be treated accordingly by the translator. The final vulgarity is the assumption that translation must take teachable form, in the end, and subserve, like a lever or a plasterer's hod, the contrivances of the classroom and the tactical labors of the grammarian. On the contrary, the whole ambience of poetry suggests that translations, like all other things that tax us with the *whole* force of their character, are literal only by expedience, and that their literalness tells us nothing at all about *poetry*. The leaf of grass that Whitman raised to his eye with the poet's cry: "What is grass?" and the poem that embodies that cry are equally tentative encounters in the history of perception; and the translator must invest each with corresponding enactments of being.

This I have tried to accomplish in the translations here assembled, with varying proximity to the original. Not all will thank me for my labors; and yet, to bring *whole* poems into my "frequency" as a translator and cope simultaneously with substantive, prosodic, and textural considerations which in the end deliver a poet *alive*, nothing less will serve. On the whole, my English translation has aimed at a line-for-line correspondence of format, except for the indentation of first lines, where I have departed from Spanish printing procedures, to suggest the contrast of traditional Spanish meters with the rhythms available in English. For those who wish to have their cake and eat it too—the usurers and bookkeepers of translation, and the sages who see the One True Translation in the middle of the air, like Ezekiel's wheel—the curve of deviation will appear perilous. It has seemed so to me, on occasion: yet I hope that the total venture of this volume will make the difference between a persistently untranslated Alberti, and an Alberti who may now begin to take shape in "selective" form and suggest the range of his accomplishment as a poet.

These remarks are quizzically and not controversially intended. They should not, for example, distract the reader from his scrutiny of the essential datum of this translation: the mind and the art and the vision of a poet already written deeply into the grain of contemporary letters and the genius of his country. We tend to look away too long from the fruits of translation, such as they are, to the theorist's concern for the criteria of translation, on the assumption that translation will wait until the issues, which are bottomless, have been resolved by an ecumenical council of pundits. But next to the community of scholars, the community of translators is perhaps the most savage of the species. One will contend that an English Neruda ought not to sound as if the translator was "writing like Shakespeare," when everyone knows Neruda should sound like a pirate. Another will invoke anonymity, piously disavowing alternatives never his to enact in the first place, and, for the best reasons in the world, lay a dead mouse at the feet of the master. Another, in the interests of "the poem itself," will follow one volume of Pushkin with three of himself, in an exegetical dazzle, like a competing soprano, in which all that was lost to the "literal" is pure *bel canto* for the critic. To each his own; I applaud the heterogeneous way; ours is a comic vocation.

[1]"Alegrías y sombras de Rafael Alberti," *Insula*, no. 198 (Madrid, May, 1963).

[2]C. M. Bowra, *The Creative Experiment* (New York: Grove Press, 1958), vii, "Rafael Alberti, *Sobre los ángeles.*"

[3]Dudley Fitts, *Poems (1929-1936)* (Norfolk, Conn.: New Directions, 1937).

[4]*La arboleda perdida*, Libros I y II (Buenos Aires: Compañía General Fabril Editora, 1959).

IV

Revaluations:

Pablo Neruda—The Oeuvre

*It's curiosity I ask
for—basic curiosity!*

8

Translator's Preface:
The Selected Poems of Pablo Neruda

T the translator of Pablo Neruda comes to his task forewarned by a poet hardened to the condescension of his detractors and the scruples of his well-wishers:

> I wrote down five verses:
> one green,
> one shaped like a breadloaf,
> the third like a house going up,
> the fourth one, a ring,
> the fifth one
> small as a lightning flash . . .
>
> Then came the critics: one deaf,
> and one gifted with tongues,
> and others and others:
> the blind and the hundred-eyed,
> the elegant ones
> in red pumps and carnations,
> others decently clad
> like cadavers . . .
> some coiled in the forehead
> of Marx or thrashing about in his whiskers;
> others were English,
> just English . . .
>
> *(Oda a la crítica)*

On the other hand, there have been many to remind us that the poetry of Pablo Neruda is in itself a species of translation. Time and again, in exploring the *Residencias*, Amado Alonso* is led to invoke the analogy of the "translator," as if to remind us of the relativism of all linguistic transactions. "So oddly ordered are the words of this poetry," he writes, "that the phrases at times seem to be translated from a foreign language and retain something of the ordering drive of the originating language." His style is described as "oneirical," "hermetic," disintegrative, wayward, irrational, surreal, and olfactory. Among the poems "shaped like bread or a ring," and those "like a house going up," we are urged to take note of eruptive and vegetal processes, intuitional configurations, images of destruction, and "the melting away of the world." On the whole, however, the genius of Neruda is torrentially affirmative, and makes a discipline of even its excesses. The stature and fascination of his vision lie in a movement of thought keyed to its own impulses and alert to its own intrinsicality, in which the successions of the verse and the successions of intuition are one and the same, and the volume and character of the feelings and fantasy serve an organic momentum, an "ascending and descending play of intensity."

The choice of the translator, in such a case, is clear; he may rest on the completed action of the poet and compile a memorandum of *words* removed from the drives of the originating excitement; or he may press for a comparable momentum in his own tongue and induce translation accordingly. It seems to be the fate of the translator always to echo the cry of Rilke's "Ninth Elegy": "Alas, but the *other relation*! What can be carried across?" and speculate mistrustfully:

> Are we, perhaps, here just for saying: House,
> Bridge, Fountain, Gate, Jug, Olive Tree, Window—
> possibly: Pillar, Tower?

The poetry of Pablo Neruda, however, is not so easily gratified. His art leaves little room for semantic optimism, or the tactical disengagement of the translator from the shock of those "other relations" which are the primary mode of its excitement. It is "ignorant" and tentative, "oceanic" and vulnerable, precisely because it postulates the enigmatic character of the substantive and communicative world. His vision, like Whitman's, is "hankering, gross, mystical, nude," but his art shows the stresses of a more protean identity, the anguish of a more unappeasable commitment. The triumph of the *oeuvre* of Pablo Neruda is to conclude,

---

Poesía y estilo de Pablo Neruda: Interpretación de una poesía hermética. Amado Alonso. (Editorial Sudamericana: Buenos Aires, 1951.)

after two decades of doctrinal idealism in which even the onion and the soup spoon are pressed into the service of dialectic, with *Estravagario*, "a book of vagaries," and a valediction which must surely concern the translator as much as it does the reader:

> I pass on to the other side of the page
> and am never lost to your sight:
> I vault through transparency,
> a swimmer of heaven,
> and return to grow
> infinitesimal, till a day
> when the wind bears me off
> and even my name is unknown to me
> and I wake to non-being;
>
> when my singing shall sound in a silence.
>
> *(Testamento de otoño)*

For all his insistence on the "poetry of the impure," the "massing of things, the use and disuse of substances," the theme of the *oeuvre* repeats Rimbaud's "je est un autre!" ("The I, is an Other"), Lorca's "Yo ya no soy yo / Y mi casa ya no es mi casa." ("I am I now no longer / And my house is no longer my house"), and the crepuscular cry of his youth: "Nosotros, los de entonces, ya no somos los mismos." ("We, we of the lapsed world, are no longer the same.")

The whole of the *Canto general (General Song)* offers a striking case in point; it is, in effect, a pageant of contrasts and metamorphoses. Here, it would seem, only the primary images of creation—Deluge, Leviathan, and the displacement of men and events that goes by the name of History —will serve to evoke the shaping purposes of the poet. Signed, in the concluding lyric, "today, 5 February, in this year of 1949, in Chile, in 'Godomar de Chena,' " it towers above the achievement of Neruda with the accumulated wealth and detritus of a lifetime. It is, like *Moby Dick* and *Leaves of Grass*—whose cadences should convey it to American ears—a *progress*: a total book which enacts a total sensibility. It moves in a framework of awe as imponderable as the cosmological figures of Job, and improvises upon the central illumination of a lifetime. It ransacks the commonplace, the topical, the singular, in its search for the generic. The premise which it seems to have served is that imagination and the political factor, the meditative life and the existential datum, comprise a single reality. In its strengths and its weaknesses, it epitomizes the double mind of messianic romanticism: the passion for the infinite and the empirical, the private fable in apocalyptical guise.

One is tempted, in casting up the sum of *Canto general*, to deal in terms of extension alone; for quantitatively, the design of the work is the most extravagant that the poetry of our time has produced. For some, like Amado Alonso, it will call to mind the "frescoes of Michelangelo"; for others, the splendors of Orozco will seem the more exact analogy. It is, in the phrase of Chesterton, a specimen of the "gigantesque." It begins at the Beginning, as a god might invoke the categories of the Creation, to fashion a habitable globe out of "Vegetation," "Some Beasts," "The Birds Arrive," "The Rivers Appear," "Minerals," "Men." It moves on to principalities, forces, powers—the "spaces of spirit" through which life looks toward death, "resurrections out of nowhere," and enters the durative factor of history.

The history is, to be sure, the American Dream as the *norteamericano* has seldom been permitted to see it—the Hispanic tradition, with Cortés, Balboa, Magellan, Bolívar, Zapata, and Juárez as its demigods, the *pampas* and capitals of Mexico and South and Central America as its theater, the perfidies and restorations of Chile as its fable, and the metamorphoses of the poet—as patriot, fugitive, exile, prophet, revolutionary, somnambulist, and bard—as its drama. It concludes, in fifteen books and 568 pages, in a veritable psalter of Isaianic salutations, with a doxology of the "Fruits of the Earth," "Wine," "Great Joy," "Death," "Life," "Testaments," "Depositions," and the divinized sign of the ego: "Yo Soy": "I Am."

A just criticism of Neruda's conception, however, would have to concern itself with less sumptuous considerations, as well. For the *Canto general*, despite its multinational address, is also a *Canto general de Chile*. Like *Leaves of Grass*, it is a work inseparable from a national scene and an identifying personality. Whatever its continental sweep and bravura, it deduces both the lyrical occasion and the vision which it serves, from the *tierra* of the poet's birth. Despite his hymns to Stalingrad, his styptic denunciations of United Fruit and Coca-Cola, his early exercises in the crepuscular and erotic French "modernist" genre, his Whitmanese, Neruda remains, in the words of Torres-Rioseco,* "the Chilean Indian from Parral."

For the North American reader, it is true, the topical exactitudes of the poet are likely to be forfeit; for this reason I have held them to a

*New World Literature: Tradition and Revolt in Latin America. Arturo Torres-Rioseco. (University of California Press. Berkeley and Los Angeles. 1949.)

minimum in this selection. Yet it is a mark of Neruda's greatness that his poetry does not wait upon historicity to deliver the imaginative and moral splendor of his theme. He transcends both the programmatic materialism of his political stance and the histrionics of his attitude. Along the fraying margins of the "political subject," Neruda moves at will from invective and reportage—from *"porfiristas* of Mexico, 'gentlefolk' of Chile, *pitucos* of the Jockey Club of Buenos Aires, the sticky filibusterers of Uruguay, Ecuadorian coxcombs, clerical lordlings of every party"—to the incandescence of the lyrical occasion. Though he is master of the Goya-esque cartoon ("The Dictators") in which compassion bites like an etcher's corrosive, he has also Whitman's capacity for moving from dimension-in-length to dimension-in-breadth-and-depth, opening the stanza to enormous increments of detail and floating the burden of the phenomenal world on the unanswerable pathos of a mystery.

Few will deny that the tyranny of the partisan position is apparent throughout the whole of this proud and obsessional book. In the end, however, it is the *"other* relation" that constantly draws the poet away from the entrenched point and the limited commitment: from "false astrologies," political slogans, and all the apparatus of historical and theoretical positivism, to the "enigmas" which have always been the "general song" of creation. The true measure of *Canto general*, despite all the labors of Neruda to make it appear otherwise, is not to be found in a place name, an artifact, or an ideological loyalty—not in Stalingrad, Lota, or Macchu Picchu—but in the "havocs and bounties" of "El gran océano," the "shattering crescents" of "Leviathan," the "fullness of time" of "Los enigmas":

> Probing a starry infinitude,
> I came, like yourselves,
> through the mesh of my being, in the night, and
>   awoke to my nakedness,
> all that was left of the catch—a fish in the
>   noose of the wind.

> (*Los enigmas*)

The present translation is offered in the spirit of this conviction; and the accomplishment may be measured accordingly. If the predicates of the "new method" urged on translators by Mr. Stanley Burnshaw in *The Poem Itself* are correct, the prevailing mood of translation is Parnassian: it is possible now to be incredulous and close quotes around the translator who *imagines* he is " 're-creating originals' "! In that case, fair warning may be more appropriate for the conscientious translator than "apology": and the reader is accordingly warned. These translations are tentative, illusionistic, and engaged. The myth of the omniscient expositor and the univocal poem has had no part in the shaping of this volume. Each word of the taxing originals, and their English equivalents, has been prayerfully meditated; yet commitment has exceeded meditation, in the end—as it must, if the result is to be a translation rather than a quandary. To keep up my courage under the assault of an identity which might otherwise have proved annihilating, I have mounted my language on rhythms which enlist the resources of poetry in English as much as they do the poetry of Pablo Neruda: I have worked at *objects*. The stresses, at times, have carried me further from the originals than I would have wished; and on certain occasions the locutions of English have tidied the syntactical disorders more than is proper. But the *Residencias* and the *Odas* are no slagpile of words! The "poem itself" remains where it always was—on "the other side of the page," where the bilingual are invited to consult it, unmediated: by translators, by schoolteachers, by critics, by polemical methodists, and by other poets.

A word with regard to the selection of a text: it should be obvious, in an *oeuvre* which already exceeds two thousand printed pages, and in which no fewer than six volumes, one of them "classic" in prestige and appeal, antedate the poet's twenty-second year, that a profile of sixty poems can hardly hope to "represent" the poet fairly. My hope has been to achieve the "representative" by other means: not by the simultaneous inclusion of set pieces from all of the volumes which comprise the complete works of Pablo Neruda, but by the projection of a diverse and mercurial talent in quest of its destiny. It has been the fate of that talent, during the last thirty-five years, to be truncated by partisan anthologists, diminished by causes, predilections, intrusions of history, injured by its own wilful insistence on allegiances which have little to do with the majesty and melancholy of its long contest with the Sphinx. There is need now to recover the true range of Neruda's labors as an agonist of the intuition: to peel away the politics, the patriotism, the provisional certainties, for that "interminable alcachofa" ("interminable artichoke") which he has called "the heart of all poets."

I say this with little hope of consoling connoisseurs in the "complete" Neruda, or devotees of any constituent part, for the omission of favorite epochs, like the youthful *Veinte poemas de amor y una canción desesperada* *(Twenty Love Poems and A Desperate Song)*, and "indispensable" international landmarks like *Qué despierte El Leñador!* *(Rail-Splitter, Awake!)* canonized by translation into the Arabian, Chinese, Slovenian, Czech, Hindu, German, French, Italian, Japanese, Russian, Polish, Rumanian, Ukrainian; and English *(Masses & Mainstream:* 1950). I offer in its place the projection of a poet working "at the right hand of power," and that poet's estimate of his true scope and commitment:

> A poetry impure as the clothing we wear, or our bodies, soup-stained, soiled with our shameful behavior, our wrinkles and vigils and dreams, observations and prophecies, declarations of loathing and love, idyls and beasts and shocks of encounter, political loyalties, denials and doubts, affirmations and taxes.

That is the order of business for a "selected poems of Neruda," and the desirable preponderance for a text. All are to be found in this volume.

9

Pablo Neruda: A Revaluation

1. THE LAUGHING NERUDA

Criticism of Neruda both in this country and South America has paid long homage to the fact—a profound, rather than a peripheral one—that whoever touches his work, touches Chile; and that ultimately, whoever touches Chile touches the whole ambience of Spanish letters. With the passing of time, however, it has become clear that appraisal has languished as well as prospered on this account; for while the achievement of Pablo Neruda has gone on crossing boundaries and denying "establishments," comment has remained singularly narrow, inbred, and positional. Too often the effect has been to decant the total essence of a much displaced identity into a "Chilean Indian from Parral," chemically inseparable from the stones, the forests, and the coastal waters of his own country. Both his admirers and his detractors dwell obsessively on particulars of Chilean landscape or Chilean politics which diminish rather than enlarge an intransigent personal vision. Compiling a long index of place-names and public occasions, they have turned a poet's dispensation to the world into a family quarrel or a South American property.

To be sure, any program which includes the *Canto general de Chile*, *Las piedras de Chile*, and *Memorial de Isla Negra*, and teems with anecdote and personal history, requires a glossary for North American readers. An overlay of continents, jungles, rivers, cities, and oceans seems to cover Neruda's world like a cartographer's isinglass; and much of *La arena traicionada*, *Crónica de 1948*, and *Las oligarquías* will require the fine print of topical Hispanists to be wholly intelligible to readers [in 1978]. Nevertheless, it is a fact that the *Canto general de Chile* was ultimately absorbed into a *Canto general*, and as the poet went on to explain: "Amidst all these visions, I wanted to paint a portrait of the struggles and victories of America as part of our very zoology and geology . . . It is a lyric attempt to confront our whole universe."[1] The true range of Pablo Neruda will never become apparent (especially to Swedish Academicians) until one has reckoned with explicit directives furnished us by his titles. His "lyric" mode embraces (1) songs (*Veinte poemas de amor y una canción desesperada*, 1924), (2) chants (*Canto general*, 1950, *Cantos ceremoniales*, 1960), (3) odes (three books of *Odas elementales*, 1954-1959), (4) sonnets (*Cien sonetos de amor*, 1959), (5) sonatas (*Sonata crítica*, 1964), and (6) barcaroles (*La barcarola*, 1968). His range is "general," "elemental," "ceremonial," and "memorial," rather than topical; and his "residence," three times over, is "on earth" (*Residencia en la tierra, I, II, III*)—or when it is not on earth, it is airy, fiery, or oceanic.

A bibliography of Pablo Neruda guides us to these key terms as surely as it detains us en route in Punitaqui, Macchu Picchu, Spain, Asia, and Isla Negra. It is to these terms, as indices to the further range of Pablo Neruda, that I should like to address myself in an introduction intended, for once, not as a translator's primer for non-Hispanic readers, but as one poet's meditation on another. I shall assume, because his essential gravity pulls the depths and meanings that way, that the poetry of Pablo Neruda is part of everything else I know and sense about work of genius everywhere; that it is not a special *barrio* or ghetto of the contemporary mind known only to the case worker and the Spanish-speaking expert in segregated mentalities; that we have wrangled too wastefully about public commitment and thought too little of the solitude of an interior stance; that his work, given "free and innocent passage," resonates against literatures other than his own, including the English, from which he has translated Blake, Joyce, and Shakespeare,[2] and that this resonance is the true measure of his long traffic with the democracy of letters.

Any revaluation of the achievement of Pablo Neruda must, I think, pause for a long, second look at a volume published after four volumes of "odes" under the fanciful title of *Estravagario* in 1958, and apparently more important to Neruda than to his critics and countrymen. Partisans of Neruda's odic and "residential" manner, fellow travelers for whom the "only" book is *Rail-Splitter, Awake!*, devotees of his *Twenty Love Poems*, and cultists of Macchu Picchu have all tended to set it aside as an interim work, like his youthful *Crepusculario* (1923)—which the oddity of its title may serve to recall. Precisely how to render the neologistic force of the title is a translator's problem which need not detain the reader for long. It is a word of prismatic obliquity, splitting the glancing illuminations of *extraviar*: to get lost, to wander off course, to divagate; *extravagante*: extravagant, eccentric, way out; *vagar*: to loiter or potter; and to English ears, at least, *vagary*, whimsy, caprice. If it is possible to call *Crepusculario* Neruda's *Book of Twilight* it may be permissible to call *Estravagario* his *Book of Vagaries*.

The titular linguistics are important only because an unplaceable word may also help to locate an unplaceable intonation and suggest the humors which invest it like an aura. The "unplaceable" factor is, indeed, something more than an aura: it is both a destination and a predicament. As "destination," its intent is to throw the complacent reader, for whom Neruda is either a monolith or a public convenience, off-course; and as a predicament, it offers a comic bath of "negative capability" in which the poet romps like a water weasel. On the one hand, his "delights are dolphin-like," and "show his back above / The element they liv'd in": on the other, they toil in the "thick rotundity of the world" for the center of a poet's disturbance, groping for transparency. Neruda's avowed penchant for "impurity,"[3] however, constantly deflects him into private caprice, a *coquetería* of unanswered solicitations, digressions of the mind's finalities into the absurd, the quizzical, and the imponderable. With good reason, he enlists the "camp" of antiquarian steel engravings from an obsolete *Works of Jules Verne*, and the "pop" of a *Book of Illustrated Objects*[4] resembling a Sears-Roebuck for the Mexican provinces, printed in San Luis Potosí in 1883. Against this iconography of persiflage, savored by a mind that shrugs away all fictions of solution, including the political, Neruda enters his defense of ignorance as an aspect of the world's redeeming impurity.

The epistemology of ignorance is the constantly augmented theme in a work which might otherwise seem a packet of damp squibs, rather than the fuse to a spiritual explosion. It begins vaguely with a cluster of unexamined intuitions: "It is dark in the mothering earth / and dark within me"; "the whole world frightens me—death and cold water"; "I am tired of the hard sea and the mysterious earth," of old hens, bad *aperitifs*, good education, statues, of concessions, of "everything well-made" and "that ages us." Who would have surmised, asks Neruda, that "earth would change her old skin in so many ways?"—with an after-thought out of Wonderland itself: "We go falling down the well of everyone else." His best hunch brings him close to the anguish of his three *Residencias*: "We are crucially alone / I propose to ask questions / let's talk man-to-man . . . No one knows what he's talking about / but all agree it is urgent."

Meanwhile, a sense of self-loss and the withering away of the known renders both question and answer increasingly remote. There is mockery as well as pathos in his clown's grimace: "My heart is so heavy / with the things that I know / it's like dragging / a dead weight of stones in a sack"; or "No matter how many we are or I am / at the moment / I can never meet up with a soul: they lose me under my clothing / they went off to some other city." At times a child's recalcitrance edges the irony of the poet's denial: "I'm not asking anyone anything / but every day I know less": "Why (do I) recognize nobody / and why does nobody recognize me?" The comedy of the amateur's stage fright, pinned down by spotlight and audience, does not escape him: "I don't know what to do with my hands / and I've thought of doing without them / —but how will I put on my ring? / What an awful uncertainty!" Sheepishly, quizzically, he calls out from his treadmill: "I don't come, I don't go / I don't dress, I don't walk about in the nude / I've thrown forks, / spoons and knives into the well. / I smile only at myself / I don't ask indiscreet questions." "Which is which, which is how?"

The true distress of the poet, however, is never far from his vagaries, and is frequently summed up in a cry: "What must I do to sort myself out? / How can I provide for myself?" The hazards of the absurd show their darkened as well as their lighted side: "A shadow moves over the earth / man's spirit is shadow / and therefore it moves." There are admonitions, cautionary asides: "I don't want to mislead myself again / it is dangerous to walk / backward, because all at once / the past is a prison." In stroboscopic changes of dark and light the poet can only assure others grimly: "From time to time, at a certain remove, / one must take one's bath in a grave"; and himself: "I'm going to open and close myself up / with my most treacherous friend, / Pablo Neruda."

The result is a parody of Socratic quest in which Neruda, committed to the "clarification of things," puts his question to priest, physician, gravedigger, and "specialists in cremation," in turn. No one will miss, under his shifting humors, macabre and impudent by turns, the shock of the poet's concussion with Death, like a roadblock barring the way to the motorist turning a curve at top speed: "The minute vanishes, vanishes

over one's shoulder," and "suddenly we have only one year to move on / a
month, a day, and death touches our calendar." The responses, as I have
tried to suggest, are riddlingly diverse, from the child's game of hide-
and-seek: "Let's count up to twelve now / Then: everyone—quiet!", to the
radiologist's glare: "Everyone sees / the plight of my shocked viscera / in
radioterrible pictures," to spiritual panic: "Help! Help! Give us a hand! /
Help us to be earthier day after day! / Help us to be / holier spray, / come
airier out of the wave!" Since finalities and outcomes are hardly germane
to a *Book of Vagaries*, the answer remains sibylline to the end: "When the
wind skims / your skull's hollows / it will show you enigmas / whispering
the truth / where your ears used to be." His ultimate impersonations are
perhaps three: "I am one who lives / in mid-ocean, close to twilight / and
further away than these stones"; "I am he who makes dreams; / in my
house of feather and stone / with a knife and a clock / I cut clouds and
waves / and out of these elements / I contrive my calligraphy."

The significance of this glancing look backward at Neruda's book of
vagaries may not yet be apparent to the casual reader. It is, in the literal
sense of the word, a pivotal book: it veers away sharply, like that "swim-
mer of heaven" in his concluding Testament, from the resolute materiality of his odes and "general songs," and "leaps into transparency." Certain
only that "those who would give me advice / become crazier with each
passing day"—including the "politically astute" who note down all
deviations, who "wrinkle, grow gray, and can't stomach their chestnuts"
—our hero of comic impurity, like the celebrated squire from La Mancha,
retires to take counsel. In full sight of the utopian dream and the "sad
countenance" of his master, he parodies his predicament with the country
humors of a yokel: "Now I don't know which way to be— / absent-
minded or respectful; / shall I yield to advice / or tell them outright
they're hysterical? / Independence, it's clear, gets me nowhere. / I get lost
in the underbrush / I don't know if I'm coming or going. / Shall I take off,
or stand firm, / pay for tomcats or tomatoes ?" His decision, in the owlish
"Parthenogenesis," is stubborn, circular, and mocking: "I'll figure out as
best I can / what I ought *not* to do—and then do it . . . If I don't make
mistakes / who will believe in my errors? . . . I'll change my whole person /
. . . and then when I'm different / and no one can recognize me / I'll keep
doing the same things that I did / since I couldn't possibly do otherwise."

Apart from the immediate drolleries of this soliloquy, which in effect
returns a rebellious Sancho Panza to the service of a dream, there would be

some somber things to say. Philosophically, it poses questions regarding the nature and uses of "advice" as a species of knowledge, about the validity of the "independent" stance as a clue to autonomous reality, about standing firm, moving off, and tactical error as a test of identity, about the changeable, the innate, and the learned. All are recognizably "existential" preoccupations, all are recklessly and joyously engaged in page after page of the *Estravagario*.

In this sense, Neruda at times comes close to the mood of his younger countryman, Nicanor Parra, with whose "anti-poems" the harlequinade of *Estravagario* has often been associated by South American critics. Certainly, it would be a mistake to overlook the affinities of the two major talents of Chile who in 1958—the year of the publication of *La Cueca Larga* and *Estravagario*—undertook to scrutinize each other at length in an exchange of *Discursos* concerned with the criteria and intent of poetry in a new decade of the South American idiom. It would be equally misleading to overlook the fact that the "anti-poem" was *always* present in the protean repertory of Pablo Neruda, in poems such as "Walking Around," from the *Residencias*, in the hard-bitten reportage of *Canto general* and the witty emaciations of the *Odas*; and that, indeed, the whole premise of an "impure" poetry invoked by Neruda in 1935 is the true precursor of the "anti-poem" both in Nicanor Parra and South American letters as a whole. The "anti-poem," after all, is an importation and not an invention of Parra's: it predates the *Poemas y anti-poemas* of Parra in the work of Corbiére, Apollinaire, Pound, Eliot, Cummings and Brecht, among others, and has been endlessly adumbrated in a genre of "anti-plays," "anti-novels," "anti-worlds," "non-essays," et cetera, which bear witness to the deflationary trend of the modern imagination in the service of the ignoble, the apostate, and the absurd. In purely Hispanic terms, it is written into the whole of *Don Quixote* where, as another avowed enemy of the baroque, Antonio Machado, liked to point out, the "Cervantine fiction" or anti-romance, calls for a "double time" and a "double space," a "twinned series of figures—real and hallucinatory . . . two integral complementary consciousnesses conversing and forging ahead" in a "book of harlequinade creating a spiritual climate which is ours to this day."

It is equally proper to suppose that the poems of *Estravagario* represent, politically, a kind of "revisionism" by a servant of good will, in the aftermath of extraordinary devotion to party lines, dogmas, tactics, and disciplines. In this case, the disengagements of *Estravagario* show both the irreverence and autonomy of Neruda's commitment to an ideology. Consulting the Presidium of his own pulses, testing the "equivocal cut of my song," he discovers he is no man's Establishment ("rector of nothing"), and in the realignment of checks and balances, opens the way to a decade of unprecedented self-scrutiny. It is to this later decade that we now turn.

2.   A HOUSE OF FOURTEEN PLANKS

Despite the prominence given it in the title and the body of the sonnets themselves, the key word of Neruda's *One Hundred Love Sonnets* (*Cien sonetos de amor*, 1959) is not "love" but "clarity" (*claridad*). The almost Parnassian abstraction of the term may jog some startled memories of the *"très-chère," "très-belle | Qui remplit mon coeur de clarté"* of Baudelaire,[5] with his equally troubled dream of a voyage under "wet suns" and "disheveled skies" to consummations where *"tout n'est qu'ordre et beauté."*[6] It is significant that, in the protean world of tidal impulses, oceanic disorder, diurnal and seasonal change which shapes the progressions of the Sonnets—Neruda's characteristic insistence upon the impurities of function and the unfolding telluric and human improvisations of a lifetime—it is *claridad* that the poet has come to espouse, literally, in the person of the Beloved.

The more closely one follows the word through the poet's calendar of "morning, afternoon, evening, and night" with its intimations of changing seasons glimpsed through the "salt disaster" of water, the "mash of the light," "all that shudders below / underfoot, underground," "the insubstantial fog," "an untimely autumn," "today, tomorrow, yesterday" that "destroy themselves in passing," the more one comes to feel its spiritual rather than its cerebral force in the poem. Only occasionally does it connect with the world of quantitative and syllogistic order, as when, viewing the Southern Cross through the "night of the human," Neruda invokes its "four zodiacal numbers" in an image of cosmological serenity. Even here, the numbers and elements connect "for a passing minute only"; the "green cross" is straightway vegetalized into parsley, animalized into fish and firefly, carbonized into diamond, absorbed into the chemistry of fermenting wine.

However imperfectly seen, it is the *claridad* of Matilde Urrutia which constitutes the poet's vision of love's permanence and the world's changes. It is Neruda's word for the beautiful—just as *integritas, consonantia, claritas* came to constitute a triad of spiritual properties of the beautiful for St. Thomas—with the special anguish of Neruda's passion for the secular way. On one hand we have the "waves' shock on unconsenting stone," "the seaweed's sodden aroma," "the towering spumes of Isla Negra"; on the other, we have the "dear Orderer" (*Ordenadora*) who "thrust[s] herself into the subterranean world," bringing definition, the "order [that] apportions its dove and its daily bread": recognizably sacramental images of providence and redemption. In between, moves the "flying hand" of the housewife, arranging cups, saucers, casseroles, "walking or running, singing or planting, sewing or cooking or nailing things down / writing, returning": and in the realm of brute nature, the tides, the breakers, the "ocean's tormented pavilions," the "machinations of the wasp / who toils in behalf of a universe of honey," and the poet's "leaky barge adrift / within a double skyline: dream and order."

The latent "religiosity" of crosses, doves, bread, wine, honey, the "crown of knives," the "scarecrow smiling his bloody smile," "mockers and backbiters," merits some passing notice, despite Neruda's wry disavowal of any "plaiting and peddling of thorns." If the doves of Sonnet LXXVIII have more in common with the doves painted by Picasso for the Second Congress of the Defenders of Peace, and if the bread is the bread written into the traditional slogans of proletarian revolt from the French Commune to the Petrograd uprisings of 1917, the special *claridad* of the Sonnets makes them resonate freshly against universal archetypes which have attended the strivings of the spirit in all ages. It is no disservice to the hard-won contemporaneity of Neruda to point out that his mystique of an "impure poetry" for engaged poets everywhere has Christian as well as existential overtones in its insistence on a "corruptible" state upon which imaginative transcendence depends. The impure, the fallen, the perishing, all that "escapes the interstices" when the net of human order has been knotted by the rational orderer, dominate the watery brooding of Neruda throughout the whole of the poet's later *oeuvre*, since the *Estravagario*.

The task of the *Cien sonetos de amor* is to retrieve an "immaculate day" in all the temporal impurity of its hours, phases, seasons, alternations of feeling and light, fixed in the last, happy *claritas* of love. On the compositional level, the labor begins with a "profanation" of the sonnet form itself, which, despite its careful count of fourteen lines apiece, omits both the end rhymes and the metrical profile which dynamize the "sonnetification" of feeling and argument, and leaves the thought to work its way through tercets and quatrains as an act of nature. Indeed, it is Neruda's intent, according to his dedicatory note to the light-and-dark lady of his sonnets, to turn the sonnet form itself *wooden*. "In proposing such a project for myself," he writes, "I was well aware that, along the edges of each [sonnet], by deliberate preference and for purpose of elegance, poets in every age have set rhymes to ring out like silver or crystal or cannon shot. In all humility, I have made these sonnets out of wood, given them the sound of that opaque and pure substance, and they should be so heard by your ears. You and I, walking through forests and sand wastes, by lost lakes and cindery latitudes, gathered those splinters of pure timber, beams delivered to the inconstancy of the water and weather. Out of the very smoothest fragments of all I have fashioned, with hatchet, penknife, and cold steel, these lumberyards of love and raised little houses of fourteen planks where your eyes, so sung and adored, may live on."

The seasoned reader of Neruda, aware of the poet's long apotheosis of wood as an image of the strenuous materiality of the world's body, will know how to make the most of this courtly compliment. The poet of the Araucanian forests who wrote:

> Whatever it is that I know
> or invoke again,
> among all the things of the world,
> it is wood that abides
> as my playfellow,
> I take through the world
> in my flesh and my clothing
> the smell
> of the sawyer,
> the reek of red boards . . .

proffers his "lumberyard of love" as confidently as sonneteers of the past have come with their more traditional nosegays and proud disavowals of marble and gilded monuments. The realism of Neruda is not pejorative. It is, however, "impure." His "century of wooden sonnets," while retaining the classical count of Quevedo and Góngora and addressing itself to themes as Petrarchan as the prosody they espouse, keep open-ended, like a paragraph of prose. Read against the tailored profiles of his great predecessors, the shagginess and waywardness of his sonnets are constantly apparent. They contract at will to the minimal beat of

Trajo el amor su cola de dolores

or spring open like a sonnet by Gerard Manley Hopkins:

No solo por las tierras desiertas donde la piedra salina

from one sonnet to the next. As little "houses of fourteen planks" unfenes-trated by end rhyme, they remain resolutely functional and unadorned: they house only large movements of the mind and show the grain and the knot of the poet's intention, rather than the scrimshaw of the prosodist's virtuosity.

On the other hand, it would be a mistake to assume that they com-prise a landscape of blockhouses and framed plank, like those pioneering encampments of the poet's childhood which went up in periodic holo-causts and were rebuilt by Temucans "who know how to build in a hurry." Viewed against the profile of the wonderfully spindled and granu-lated *Odes*—or indeed, from any vantage point along the circumference of poetry as such—his "century of sonnets" registers with remarkable ele-gance as a city of the mind in which passion and meditation come and go with powerful strides toward a noble objective. Indeed, it is with some-thing of surprise that one comes to realize—as an afterthought, rather than a concession to the "rail-splitting" Neruda—that the customary stabilizers and parquetry of sonnet are not regularly present in the unfold-ing poem. This is due, in part, to the "feminine" genius of latinate discourse as such, with its functional repetition of identical or assonantal slack syllables which makes it almost impossible, at least to Anglo-Saxon ears, for Italian and Spanish not to *seem* to rhyme.

Closer reading reveals, however, the deeply traditional source of both the eloquence and the concord of the *Sonnets*. The density of a quatrain like the following, for example, should be apparent even without the translator's gloss:

Ay de mí, ay de nosotros, bienamada,
sólo quisimos sólo amor, amarnos,
y entre tantos dolores se dispuso
sólo nosotros dos ser malheridos.

The eloquence is there because the elegance is there, the traditional rhetoric of invocation and lament balancing romantic outcry with Gongoristic refinement, parallel syncopation of key words: *sólo*, *nosotros*, *amada*, *amarnos*. In Sonnet LXVI, where all is sparely set on the bones of the sonnet, and end rhyme is regular, Neruda proves that he can, at will, produce a sonnet in the classical vein of the Spanish masters, where the combining elements—marked density, parallelism, repetition, and a "Shakespearean" prosody so adroitly fused with the "Italianate" as to create a continuous texture of two end rhymes used six and eight times respectively—all point the way to the sources in Quevedo and Góngora so highly esteeemed by the poet.

On the whole, the effect of Neruda's constant *sauvización* of the lines is to exchange the rail-splitter's hatchet for the eloquence of the cabinet-maker and the artisan. The fact that the eloquence is virile, flexible, intimate, need deceive no one, just as his earlier identification with Lincoln as railsplitter (*El Leñador*) and Vallejo as "carpenters, poor carpenters," is inseparable from his compositional integrities as an artist. The *Cien sonetos de amor* are a landmark in the literature of the sonnet that confirms again the catholicity of Neruda's genius at its flood tide, at the same time that it breathes new life into dry sticks. It accomplishes the miracle of transforming that most servile and feudal of forms—the sonnet's long complaint of knightly self-denial and court compliment contrived for the express delectation of a patron—into a husband's book of hours, grievances, privacies, troubled meditations. It removes the inamorata, once coy and cruel by turns, from her medieval tower, into the kitchen, with its recognizably bourgeois panoply of "cups and glasses / cruets of oil and oleaginous golds," sets her, sharp as a snapshot, against a background of "blue salt, with the sun on the breakers," as she emerges, "mother-naked . . . taking her place in the world." It eternizes her in "ovens of clay with Temuco adobe," without the Renaissance boast of indestructibility for "this scribbling on the paper." In its fusion of both the elegant and the immediate, it proves again the eventual sophistication of Neruda's premise of the Impure as a species of "pastoral," in which, as Empson once pointed out, the complex man goes to school to the simple man "to mirror more completely the effective elements of the society he lived in."[7]

3.   THE MOURNING NERUDA

The year 1961-1962 is notable, in Neruda's long chronicle of plenty, for the publication of three volumes of verse, each differing from the other in form and subject matter, and all in marked contrast to the special rigors of the *Sonnets: Las piedras de Chile (The Stones of Chile), Cantos ceremoniales (Ceremonial Songs),* and *Plenos poderes (Full Powers). The Stones of Chile,* which the poet with good reason calls his "flinty book," not only follows the format of a volume by Pierre Seghers celebrating the stones of France, with photographs by Antonio Quintana, but, we are told in a preface, was "twenty years in my mind." During those years, Neruda contemplated the coastland of Chile with its "portentous presences in stone," which he later transformed "into a hoarse and soaking language, a jumble of watery cries and primordial intimations." The result is a "memorial" which organizes Neruda's lifelong fascination with the craggy, the telluric, and the metallurgical into a veritable Stonehenge of exact and monumental fantasy. The dimensions and intensities shift from poem to poem and image to image, from gigantic evocations in the vein of *Macchu Picchu,* to pebbles for the passing delight of a child, to memorial cairns and barrows elegizing the metamorphoses and convulsions of geological time. This is no mere programmatic picture book of curiosities, however, ready-made for the sightseer—no tourist's guide to the stones of Chile as "house," "harp," "hairy ship," "big table," or a bestiary of playful petrefactions including a bull, an ox, a lion, a turtle, and three ducklings. It is a free-hand lithography of time and the spirit.

In any other hands, *The Stones of Chile* might well have turned into a marginal rather than a residual book, a mineralized eschatology. What is remarkable is the speed and the certainty with which Neruda, working in sportive and approximate contexts—the profiles which distance and illusion confer on stones—divines a deeper subject twenty years in the making, like antediluvian artifacts in the "corings" of a geologist. The poet's *aficiones* for wood, water, cereals, stars, shells, are already well-known staples of his substantive world, manifestations of his deep purchase on the "impure." His essay on "oceanography,"[8] with its spacy trajectory from the Pillars of Hercules to the *krakens* of Copenhagen and the *narwhals* of the North Sea, his conchologist's passion for the artifacts of the sea floor, his delight in plankton and the sea horse (rendered doubly attractive by the Spaniard's whimsical equivalence: *"unicornio marino"*) similarly confirm his passion for the oceanic. *The Stones of Chile* takes a titan's step forward to fix them all in a massive *assemblage* of images, Medusan in its genius for turning to stone all it gazes upon.

The result, curiously enough, is not frozen Heraclitus or stopwatched Bergson, but a set of poems which yield to the imagination at every turn:

which breathes, dissolves, nourishes like those visceral deposits secreted by the ambergris whale so often observed by the poet from his Isla Negra window.[9] Nothing is less static or earthbound than the stones of Neruda's Chile: by his "Great Rock Table" the "child that is truth in a dream / and the faith of the earth" waits "for his portion"; in his Harp, nothing moves but "a world's lonely music / congealing and plunging and trying its changes"; his Ship sails placelessly through deaths and distances; and out of his Blind Statue, he "cut[s] through the stone / of my joy toward . . . the effigy shaped like myself," devising "hands, fingers, eyes." Caliban's world of rock and primordial ooze is transformed into Ariel's domain of light, speed, scintillations, island music, ether:

> In the stripped stone
> and the hairs of my head
> airs move
> from the rock and the wave.
> Hour after hour, that changing of skins,
> the salt in the light's marination.

Despite the frequently "hoarse and soaking language," the "jumble of watery cries and primordial intimations," the impact of the volume is neither sodden nor wooden. Its contour remains, as it should, sculptural, mobile, diaphanous: "weddings of time and the amethyst," "marriages of snow and the sea" which mirror "the heart's whole transparency / in / the boulder / the water."

By contrast, the *Ceremonial Songs*, also dated 1961, is a more diverse work than either the book of sonnets or the book of stones. The title at once directs us to a difference of tempo, scale, intonation. In opting for the "ceremonial," certainly, Neruda is removing himself from the "general"—a designation he was happy to claim for that heroic compendium embracing fifteen volumes and 568 pages in the original edition published in 1950 (*Canto general*). Since the poet himself does not dwell on the "ceremonial" factor as such, one is left to deduce its attributes from a scrutiny of the constituent songs: their content, their form, the whole ambience of the "ceremonious" inflection. One notes, first of all, that it is a book which deals in sequences, concatenations, trains of poems, rather than "taciturn castles"[10] of stone or "little houses of fourteen planks";[11] it is a book of long poems—the longest in twenty-two sections and the shortest in four—of a decidedly meditative and exploratory cast. The subjects fall readily into four general categories: commemorative pieces devoted to literary and historical personages (Manuela Sáenz, lover of Simon Bolívar; de Lautréamont); seasonal pieces, embracing midsummer and the rainy season; landscapes (Spain, Cádiz, the cordilleras of Chile, the ocean); and introspective pieces like "Cataclysm" and "Party's End," in which the poet contemplates his world, his person, and his scruples with a characteristic rotation or circuition of the troubled matters it contemplates.

The range of *Ceremonial Songs*, then, is ambitious: there is no attempt on the poet's part to mitigate the gravity and duration of his inductive labors. On the contrary, it seems to be one of the shaping criteria of the "ceremonial" that it aggrandizes and solemnizes whatever it touches. To be "ceremonious," apparently, is to be formal, speculative, unhurried: to build more and more *time* into the unfolding of the mind's apprehension of itself. In the realm of content, it is also, clearly, to celebrate and to elegize. However diversely the subject veers from persons to places, and from places to the things which embody them, the unity of mood, temper, tone, throughout the *Ceremonial Songs*—a kind of spiritual seepage—remains inviolable to the end.

At first reading, the persisting factor is felt to be a pervasive melancholy; but successive rereadings fix the melancholy as profoundly elegiac in origin. Only by adding the elegiac weight of the *Ceremonial Songs* to the cosmic and erotic melancholy of the sonnets and the book of stones, can one begin to intimate the distinguishing cachet of the later poetry of Pablo Neruda. What remains to be noted in the whole vista of the late Neruda, from its whimsical inklings in *Estravagario* to the processional densities of *La Barcarola*;[12] is the *de-ideologizing* of his subject, and its nervy containment in immediate acts of the poet's mind: his increasing reluctance to terminate existing doubts by rational acts of the will. It is this that imparts to all the hopes, apprehensions, positional assurances of the poet, their penumbral melancholy. And it becomes the task of "ceremony" to mediate between melancholia and the world, summoning up what is left of the old dispensation and casting out despair by re-imagining the real in existential rather than ideological terms.

In short, the "ceremonial" songs serve notice that we have to do with a *mourning* Neruda, a *"poeta enlutado"*: not in the pusillanimous guise which Neruda rejects both for himself and a perishing world ("The stones do not mope!") but the mourning once deemed "becoming" to Elektra, orphaned exemplar of the world's kinship. Certainly it would be a disservice to suggest that the "mourning Neruda," like the "music-practising Socrates,"[13] is not sustained and consoled at every turn by political particulars which, in the striker's militant parlance of the '30's, *organize* in the midst of mourning. Indeed, nothing is more apparent in the spectrum of Neruda's labors as poet and humanist than the energizing genius of both his melancholy and his empirical anguish. On the other hand, the abiding presence of the *poeta enlutado*—to which he testifies everywhere without guile or reservation—is equally apparent as a constant of his imaginative sensibility. If, in 1924, he begins with a ratio of "twenty love poems" to "one desperate song" (*Veinte poemas de amor y una canción desesperada*), the evidence of his work throughout the three *Residencias* makes it clear that the desperate song was actually unending, and determined the "surrealistic" displacements eventually wrought by his prerevolutionary acedia. ("It so happens I'm tired of just being a man.") And if, as Luis Monguió has suggested,[14] the emergent politics of Neruda turns the world's melancholy into a celebration in which "*every* song is a love song," the seminal reciprocities of love and melancholy remain significant.

A sampling of the progressions of the most ingratiating of the pieces will serve to illustrate both the tactics and the dynamics of the "ceremonial": *Fin de fiesta* / *Party's End*—the terminal book of the poem as a whole. To all intents and purposes, the occasion of this vortical poem in thirteen parts is scenic and seasonal: the "first rains of March," the sea-coasts of Isla Negra, and the omnipresent changes of the Ocean. Underneath this amalgam, however, like a tidal force under a breaker, a deeper theme asserts itself: the confrontation of renewable nature with unrenewable man. It manifests itself first in the motif which gives the poem its ironically lackadaisical title: the theme of "*fiesta*." By "fiesta," it appears, Neruda intends the gregarious drive that assembles, celebrates, and eventually disperses all things—not merely the single "reveler," but the corporate being of his "words and mouths," the "roads," by which he materializes and disappears. By Section Two, the poet has accomplished a kind of symbiotic fusion of the Season, the Man, and the Festival, into a single aspect of the world's temporality.

The motifs of seasonal rain and the sea return in Section Three, "exploding in salt," ebbing, delaying, "leaving only a glare on the sea," and are churned into a "spray" of eschatological wonderment. On the one hand, the "submerged things" of the universe ask: "Where are we going?" and on the other, the algae riding the currents ask: "What am I?" They are answered by "wave after wave after wave," with Heraclitean enigmas: "One rhythm creates and destroys and continues: / truth lies in the bitter mobility."

The word "bitter" (*"amargo"*) is a clue to the encompassing melancholy that thereafter seeps into the matrix of the piece and turns all into an elegiac meditation on the efficacy of human exertion—the people, footprints, dead papers, "transportation expenses" (*"gastos de transportes"*) of man's efforts to match the unkillable being of the world with acts of the will and imagination. Here the weariness of the poet is such that he asks for a suspension, if not indeed a liquidation, of the inhabited world: inhabited poems, inhabited beaches, inhabited time, where the "habitable" is construed as the "distinguishing mark" of individual initiative: "for a moment let no living creature enter my verse." For the first time since the *Residencias* of his youth, Neruda, looking away from causes, factions, ideological commitments, into the void where the crystal expands, the rocks climb the silence, and the ocean "destroys itself," restates that heresy of all engaged protagonists: "It so happens I'm tired of just being a man." A more haunting issue, apparently, has presented itself with his returning acedia: it is Antony's enigma of the "marring of energy," and the miracle by which "the ocean destroys itself without marring its energy." The quantitative anguish of things is summed up by Neruda in another outcry, which measures the inadequacy of a world in which "our fathers in patches and hand-me-downs . . . entered the warehouses as one entered a terrible temple": the consumer's outcry of *How much?*

Thus, a third of the way into a shifting and many-sided poem, the backlash of baffled intentionality reasserts itself in political and polemical terms. A new insistence on expedient protestation—on "the whithers and wherefores / wherever it pleases me—from the throne to the oil-slick / that bloodies the world," mounting as the "grains of my anger grew greater," turns the purchaser's *How much?* into the prophet's and the revolutionary's *How long?* There follows another turn of the poet's imagination as a new assault of personal choice on the inequalities of the human condition flows into the voids and pockets of his initial melancholy. It is this systole-diastole of his meditative patterns that is the distinctive mark of the "mourning and organizing" Neruda. Indeed, he seems to breathe as naturally as a sponge on the ocean floor of his exacerbated discomfiture. He absorbs doubts, contradictions, passing flotsam in the great baths of ricocheting images and uneasy afterthoughts which he inhabits, rocking in the play of altering pressures, volumes, thermal densities, speeds. No one has written more vividly than Neruda of the thermodynamics and psychology of the deep-sea diver (See "Ode to A Diver"[15]); and somewhere, at the critical depths which break or sustain the human violator of the oceanic and the subterranean, Neruda has known how to anchor the rational balances which turn chaos into meditative order.

The result is an elegiac poem not unlike the *Elegien* of Rilke in both the discontinuities of its empirical search for hard answers, its preoccupation with "the dead with the delicate faces," the "preciously dead,"[16] and its insistence on "clarity," joy, a strenuous humanism which asks nothing of "angels" in its pursuit of the heart's fears and the spirit's intimations. It differs from Rilke's "ceremonial" amalgam of melancholy, skepticism, and temporal love, of course, in its *visceralization* of thought—its commingling of thought with "the thorn's languages / the bite of the obdurate fish / the chill of the latitudes / the blood on the coral / the night of the whale"—and its pendulum backswing toward "men." The *"Engel-nicht— Menschen-nicht"* ("Not men, not angels"[17]) of Rilke's impasse, glimpsed only briefly in Section Four, is promptly exchanged for "the brutal imperative . . . that makes warriors of us, gives us the stance / and inflection of fighters," as Neruda crosses his "bridge of commitment" (*lo que hicimos*) into the "pride of a lifetime" and its "organized splendor" (*el esplandor organizado*).

If the accomplishment of Neruda in *Party's End*, however, were merely tactical and ideological, one might well prefer to sweep backward to the derogated Rilke for truer confrontations of the human condition. The triumph of *Party's End*, however, is that its oceanic circuits stay nowhere for long, are not positional. The day sought by Neruda, in the end, is neither paradisiac nor ideological: it is an "expendable day," "a day bringing oranges," rather than a day of reckoning—though some hint of the social dream clings to the afterthought: "the day / that is ours if we are there to retrieve it again." At the close of the poem, the "white spindrift," the "ungratified cup of the sky," the "watery autumn" move in again, and with them, the obdurate mobilities of a poet who remains "just as I was / with my doubts, with my debts, / with my loves / having a whole sea to myself." Apparently, it has been enough to "come back," to touch his "palms to the land," to "have built what I could / out of natural stone, like a native, open-handed," to "have worked with my reason, unreason, my caprices, / my fury and poise." No longer "deracinate" (*sin mis raices*) as man, as poet, as Chilean, clouded and luminous by turns, Neruda can now

> . . . say: "Here is my place," stripping myself down in
>   the light
> and dropping my hands in the sea,
> until all is transparent again
> there under the earth, and my sleep can be tranquil.

This redistillation of serenity clings to the whole of Neruda's *Plenos poderes* (1962), imparting to each of the thirty-six poems that unmistakable "fullness of power" to which its title bears witness. Weary "neither of being nor of nonbeing," still "puzzling over origins," professing his old "debts to minerality," yet wavering "as between two lost channels under water," the poet "forges keys," "looks for locks," opens "broken doors," pierces "windows out to living." What was plaintive or suspended in the *Ceremonial Songs* brightens in the up-beat of re-examined commitment, for which Neruda's distinguishing word is *"deberes"*: obligations, and its ancillary variations in *deber*: ought, should, must, owe. Thus, in the introductory poem entitled *"Deberes del poeta"* ("The Poet's Obligations"), his concern is less with possibility than with necessity—the imperatives freely imagined and professed by the poet, to which Yeats gave the name of "responsibilities." The options subsumed under the "responsible" are at once explicit and mysterious: "I must hear and preserve without respite / the watery lament of my consciousness," "I must feel the blow of hard water / and gather it back in a cup of eternity," "I must encounter the absent," I must tell, I must leave, journey, protect, become, be, eat, and possess. Elsewhere, the poet alludes to the "responsibility of the minute hand," the accumulation of "persons and chores," "the imperious necessity for vigilance," "lonely sweetnesses and obligations," "mineral obligations," and "obligations intact in the spume." These, the poet explains, are compelled upon him "not by law or caprice, / but by chains: / each new way was a chain"; he calls for "caution: let us guard the order of this ode," but his mood is blithe: "I am happy with the mountainous debts / I took on . . . the rigid demand on myself of watchfulness / the impulse to stay myself, myself alone . . . my life has been / a singing between chance and resiliency."

Side by side with the theme of resiliency (*la dureza, la dura realidad*), goes a theme of *pureza*, purity, as both a measure of the poet's effectiveness and a reward of his happy "obligation." A table of variations would include not only a multitude of passing allusions—pure waves, pure lines, pure towers, pure waters, pure bodies, pure hearts, pure feet, pure salts—and their variants in *claro* (clear lessons, clear capitals, clear vigilance, as well as "clarities" that are smiling, cruel, and erect) but entire poems like *"Para lavar a un niño"* ("To Wash A Child") and *"Oda para planchar"* ("In Praise of Ironing"). All, says the poet, must be cleansed, washed, whitened, made clear: as in a Keatsian dream of "pure ablution round earth's human shores,"[18] the land's outline is washed by the salt (*sal que lava la línea*) and the land's edge washes the world (*La línea lava el mundo*). Not only does Neruda invoke "a time to walk clean" in the name of the newly washed infant, and insist on "ironing out" the whiteness of the sea itself (*hay que planchar el mar de su blancura*); in the end poetry itself is made white: (*la poesía es blanca*).

Thus, between *dureza* and *pureza* (resiliency and purity) and *deberes* and *poderes* (obligations and powers) the poet "writes [his] book about what I am" (*escribo un libro de lo que soy*) with stunning mastery of all the themes which embody a total identity. The "mourning carpenter" (*enlutado carpintero*) of *Estravagario* and the *Sonnets* is still there, "attending the casket, tearless, / someone who stayed nameless to the end / and called himself metal or wood": he contributes two of the volume's eulogies, one addressed to the dead "C.O.S.C." and the other, to the nine-and-a-half-year old "little astronaut" whose "burning car" touches "Aldabaran, mysterious stone," and "crosses a life line." The old preoccupations with the lost and remembered of a poet bemused by the sacramental character of all change are found again in poems like "The Past" (*"Pasado"*); and the old melancholy ("To Sorrow," *"A la tristeza"*): "For a minute, for / a short life, / take away my light and leave me / to realize / my misery, my alienation." So, too, are the dead, "the poor dead (*al difunto pobre*), the people (*el pueblo*), the nights and the flora of Isla Negra (*Alstromoería, la noche de Isla Negra*), farewells (*adioses*), births (*los nacimientos*), ocean, water, sea, planet, tower, bird—each lending new force to that fullness of power by virtue of which a master of chiaroscuro "in the full light of day" paradoxically still "walks in the shade."

4. THE BURNING SARCOPHAGUS

The great watershed of the sixth decade of Pablo Neruda—the work which, at the present writing, soars like the terminal pylon of a bridge spanning four epochs including the *Residencias*, *Canto general*, and the *Odas*—is, of course, the *Black Island Memorial* (*Memorial de Isla Negra*), published in 1964 to solemnize the poet's sixtieth birthday. In effect, it constitutes a fourth gargantuan span over which flows the spiritual traffic of more than half a century, on its way to destinations as hazardous and uncharted as those previously inhabited by a poet who warns us:

> I have never set foot in the countries I lived in,
> every port was a port of return:
> I have no post cards, no keepsakes of hair
> from important cathedrals.

Its trajectory supports the weight, the diversity, and the architectural stresses of everything encountered en route: exile, deracination, embattled ideologies, and the vested enmity of the world. All that the poet has written, imagined, foresuffered in purgatorial changes of forms and allegiances: shapes of the "crepuscular," the erotic, the tentative, the "enthusiastic," halfway houses of wood and stone, and "residences" that metamorphose into bloody bivouacs in Spain, consulates in Rangoon, Ceylon, India, Mexico, France, flights into Russia, China, Mexico, Peru, "voyages and homecomings" to his native cordilleras—all the wanderings of Ishmael and The Prodigal Son, debouch like a great estuary into the pages of *Black Island Memorial*, from whose terminus "Casa La Chascona,"[19] a poet's "house of dishevelment," arises like a hand-hewn Acropolis.

One puts the case a little grandly because the poet's conception is almost orientally pyramidal in its vision of a monument built by the living for a residence *not* of this earth, as well as on it. *Black Island Memorial* is a chieftain's or a pharaoh's personal cenotaph, calling to mind the *alcazares* of Andulucía and the Heorots of Anglo-Saxon myth, hung with shields, talismans, shaggy animal pelts and precious stones, whalebone curiosities of the "seafarer" and "far-wanderer," and encircled by the ocean like a moat. How barbarously or how cunningly Neruda has built his vast *Memorial*, what artifacts, prophecies, legends and gods he has carried over his hearthstone, what enigmas still await him in island, mainland, and ocean, remain to be examined.

The critic's first task, confronted with the grandeurs and *longueurs* of this conception, must be a qualitative one: how to align the "memorial" with the "general," the "elemental," and the "ceremonial" as four phases in the orientation of a talent. I should like first of all to suggest that the "memorial" mode is *nonhistorical*: in Coleridge's words, it "emancipates [the poet] from the order of time and space,"[20] whereas the general, the elemental, and the ceremonial may be subsumed under it as modes and dimensions of the temporal. The dynamic that gave *Canto general* its unwearying sweep and thrust after three anguished *Residencias*, was history: history as the court chronicler and the anthropologist conceive it, and History as the polemical Marxist conceives it in an escalating dialectic of freedom and bondage. It is the historical mode, in this layman's understanding of the term, that induced Neruda to join his private chronicle with the perfidies and restorations of Chile, and the Creation story with a multinational saga of the death of kings, conquistadors, quislings, duces, and assorted "satraps" in a Century of Perishing Capital. His chronicle is roughly vertical in its sequences: into its rational progressions stream real wars, personal memoir, autobiography, topical villains and saviors, political reportage, global and national disasters, up to the final page, signed, in the poet's own hand, "today, 5 February, in this year / of 1949, in Chile, in 'Godomar / de Chena,' a few months before / the forty-fifth year of my life."

The pentad of Isla Negra, on the other hand, is concerned with memory rather than history. Into its five volumes there tumble a disorganized *recherche* of events, ruminations, obsessive image, words, doubts, allegiances, political mandates and spiritual recoils in an *ordre du coeur* rather than an *ordre raisonné*. Their point of departure and their point of return are essentially the same: *time present*, in which the poet, brooding daily on the change and the permanence of things from a seacoast in Isla Negra, is induced to evoke an answering dialectic from within. The dialectic is not Marxian, but metaphysical, and its polarizing genius is not History but Memory—the same power invoked by St. Augustine as "the belly of the mind"[21] in Book X of the *Confessions*. The scene, for all its flashbacks into the displacements of a lifetime, is Isla Negra, to whose sea changes, cloudscapes, and seasonal immediacies the poet constantly returns for a "residence on earth" fixed at last by the heart's choice and due process of mortality.

Visitors to Isla Negra have, between jest and earnest, alluded increasingly to the islanded Neruda as Buddha, guru, and lama[22]—a kind of Latin amalgam of Merlin and Prospero. More often than not, the epithets are irreverently, if affectionately, intended: but the "saintly" Neruda, with his unflinching gaze on the "four perturbations of the mind:[23] desire, joy, fear, sorrow" and his Augustinian assault upon Memory, is an exact distillation of the impact of the *Memorial*. Coming into "the plains, caves, and caverns of my memory" from the secular engagements of a lifetime, he says, almost in Augustine's words ("There meet I with myself and recall myself, and when, where, and what I have done, and under what feelings"):

> I also would see myself coming
> and know in the end how it feels to me
> when I come back to the place where I wait for myself
> and turn back to my sleep and die laughing.

The laughter of Neruda is a special dimension of the Hispanic—the Cervantine gift of the *quixotic*, in the presence of the Impossible, as it has flowed into the parlance of the world from the uplands of La Mancha. Like both Quixote and Augustine, however, Neruda is called back, out of History to the "reasons and laws innumerable of numbers and dimensions, none of which hath any bodily sense impressed," and to the "deeper recesses" where "all must be drawn together again, that they may be known; that is to say, they must as it were be collected together from their dispersion"; and, indeed, "re-collected." Thus, we have Neruda's:

> *Memory*
>
> All must be remembered:
> a turning wind, the threads
> in the threadbare event must be gathered,
> yard after yard of all we inhabited,
> the train's long trajectory,
> the trappings of sorrow.
>
> Should a rosebush be lost
> or the hare's track dissolve in the night,
> should the pillars of memory
> topple out of my reach,
> I must remake the air,
> the steam and the soil and the leaves . . .

> I was always an avid forgetter:
> in my two human hands
> only the untouchable things of the world
> live unscathed,
> and the power of comparison
> is the sum of their total destruction.

Forgetting, destroying, comparing, the human rememberer, "toiling in the heavy soil" of his being, like Augustine, discovers not sequence and consequence, but the plasm of identity itself, the ego which has been the subject of the poet's wonder in Whitman, in Hopkins, in Neruda, and Aurelius Augustinus of Tagaste and Carthage. "What is nearer to me than myself?" asks Augustine. "It is I myself who remember, I the mind." Ransacking the world of "things, either through images, as all bodies, or by actual presence," he comes upon the mind's own testament of what it has committed to memory, "that same memory where before [all] lay unknown, scattered, and neglected." Augustine has suggested the exaltation and despair of the chase, with Nerudian avidity: "Over all these do I run, I fly; I dive on this side and on that, as far I can, and there is no end . . . Thus do I remember Carthage." And Eliot in our own century has nodded acerb consent: "To apprehend / The point of intersection of the timeless / With time, is an occupation for a saint."[24]

This I take to be both the task of Neruda's *Memorial*, and a measure of its "sanctity" for which no fashionable mystique need be sought. Again and again, over the record of personal loves, circumstantial and topical particulars, names, dates, habitations, concretions, a persisting query is heard, turning the knowable into a "dangerous world"[25] of wandering lights and haunted misgivings: "Who was I? What? What were we both?" In a poem taking its title directly from Blake's great archetype of spiritual quest, "Little Boy Lost," Neruda suggests the malaise of the saintly identity:

> Nothing answers me now: let it pass.
> *Being* never was once: we went on being . . .
> All kept on happening,
> one man impurely persisting,
> son of the purely born son,
> till nothing remained as it was . . .
> Sometimes we remember
> the presence that lived with us,

there is something we want from him—that he remember
     us, maybe,
or know, at least we were he and now talk
with his tongue,
but there in the wreckage of hours
he looks at us, acknowledging nothing.

The note is sounded again, plangent and ardent by turns, in "Those Lives":

"That's how I am," I'll say, leaving this
pretext in writing. "This is really my life."
But everyone knows that's not how it happens at all.
Not only the cords in the net, but the air
that escapes the interstices matters:
The rest remains as it was: inapprehensible.

and again:

I live as I can
in my destiny's ruthless lucidity,
between the luminous and the desperate halves,
disowned
by two kingdoms which never were mine.

and again:

Who is that Other I am? He who never
contrived how to smile and died of his perfect deprival?
Who outlasted the festival bells and the gala
carnation, and toppled the lecterns of cold?

Late, it grows late. I go on with it all. I pursue
this or that paradigm, never guessing the answer,
knowing myself, in each of the lives I have lived,
both absent and present, at once the man who I was,
     and I am.

Does the rub of mysterious verity lie there?

The quest for "mysterious verity" is constant throughout these volumes of palpable and impalpable stock-taking, jarring all that clings to the poet's ego, from its moorings in the historical past. In the "memorial" world of Isla Negra, the poet's *verdad* is exactly equivalent to the lover's search for *claridad* in the *Sonnets*—with which it is eventually fused. Keeping "steadfastly triangular," seeing all "at first hand," affirming the "power of the real to augment / and enlarge us," yet "cherish[ing] the equivocal cut of my song," Neruda writes "on the card of our hunger / an order of bread and an order of soul for the table." For this purpose, he returns to that most elusive and obsessive of this themes: the Song of Myself, and its complementary theme of Non-Being—the *Ser-y-no-ser*, the *Nada*, and the *Sueño* that link him to the great Hispanic tradition of self-contemplation in Calderón, in Unamuno, in Machado, in Guillén. It is in his unappeasable self-absorption, from *Twenty Love Poems and a Desperate Song*, up to the present—his solipsistic meditation on the "water and rock" of "realism and idealism, both parts of my world"—that his love and his desperation have their source.

A closer look at the first of the five volumes of his *Memorial* may help to illustrate. It begins, as did the concluding section of *Canto general* (flamboyantly entitled *Yo soy: I Am*) twenty years before, with a retrospective account of the childhood and the young manhood of the poet. The title of the present volume, however, focuses upon a habitation rather than a name, on a landscape rather than an ego: Temuco of the alternate droughts and rains, the earthquakes, the timberlands, the holocausts— *Donde nace la lluvia (Where the Rain Begins)*. In his singularly appealing essay on "Childhood and Poetry," published in 1954,[26] ten years before his *Memorial*, Neruda has given us a prose recitative for his Song of Temuco: a personal history from the days of his great-great-grandparents who planted their vines in Parral, to the remarriage of his father, "a nondescript farmer, a mediocre laborer, but a first-class railroader," and his removal to Temuco.

It would appear that Neruda has deliberately set out, in *Where the Rain Begins*, to produce a versified "Childhood and Poetry"—a kind of Wordsworthian *Prelude* to a chronicle of wanderings and revolution, over which the "Spirit of the Place" broods to the end, as the Lake Country broods over the musings of Wordsworth. Where the prose chronicler informs us, for example, that "My mother could pick out in the dark, among all the other trains, precisely the train that was bringing my father into the Stationhouse at Temuco or taking him away," the Spirit of the Place remembers: "The brusque father comes back / from his trains: / we could pick out / his train whistle / cutting the rain, a locomotive's / nocturnal lament / in the dark. Later / the door started trembling." The plank houses, alternately soaking and burning, the mother "dead in Parral not long after I was born," the "tutelary angel" of his father's remarriage, Doña Trinidad Candia, the "glacial" cold of the Temucan schoolhouse, the midsummer forays into the Araucanian forests, the "searing" Cautín and the summits of Nielal, the swans of Lake Budi, the green plums, the beetles, the *copihues*, the secret world of Sandokan and Sandokana,[27] and above all, the omnipresent whistle of the night train cutting fatefully through flood, distances, and darkness with the wail of a vanished paternity—all are transcribed from the essayist's pages.

Here, it would appear, History and Memory are well matched. The way is vertical, if circuitous, and the elements are in sequence: Birth, First Journey, The Stepmother (*La Mamadre*), The Father, The First Ocean, The Southern Earth, Winter School, Sex, Poetry, Timidity, Swan Lake—such, literally, is the order of his book. Precisely when all is in readiness for a triumphal affirmation of consciousness, however, the Spirit of the Place materializes like a wraith to reaffirm the poet's total disbelief in the buoyant historicity of his chronicle. The pivot which triggers his melancholy significantly takes its title from the poem by Blake already referred to: "Little Boy Lost" (*"El niño perdido"*) and the theme of loss— *"lo perdido"*—is thereafter never absent from the long circuit of the *Memorial*. As it happens, the word is one of the most multiple—and therefore least translatable—in the rich overlay of its contexts in Spanish. Beginning somewhat lamely with its nominal denotation—"lost"—it traverses an equivocal spectrum from "vanished," "absent," "lapsed," "destroyed," "forgotten," "fallen," to "dead"—always with a nostalgic look backward. Its blood cousin, the multifaceted word to which it generally points, like a needle to a magnet, is *soledad*, or aloneness, loneliness, isolation, self-engrossment, intactness, alienation. Between, whirls a mob of grieving mutations: *confuso* (confused), *secreto* (secret), *indeciso* (indecisive), *enlutado* (mournful)—the *no-sé-qué* (I-don't-know-what) of empirical metaphysics on its way to the limbo of the *No-Ser* (Non-Being).

A sampling of the pages of *Where the Rain Begins* must suffice to suggest both the persistence of the lost (*lo perdido*) and its absorption into the spectrum of the solitary (*soledad*). There are *pasos perdidos* (lost footsteps), *fiebre o alas perdidas* (lost fever or wings), *bodega perdida entre las trenes* (shop lost among trains), *grité perdido* (I cried out, lost), *se perdía mi infancia* (my childhood was lost), *perdí los arboles* (I lost the trees), and the *estudiante triste perdido en el crepúsculo* (sad schoolboy lost in the twilight)—which brings the poet up to the publication of his second volume, *Crepuscvlario, The Book of Twilight.* In between, glows an *ignus fatuus* of flickering modulations which are the special illumination of the memory asserting its bafflement at the intersection of time with the time-less. Here, too, the contexts are diverse: *se me confundo los ojos y las hojas* (my eyes and the leaves are confused), *la confusa soledad* (the confused solitude), *una luz indecisa* (an indecisive light), *entro indeciso* (I enter undecided), *la enlutada noche* (the mournful night), *yo, enlutado, severo, ausente* (I, mournful, severe, absent), *volví con el secreto* (I returned with the secret), *en el secreto mundo / caminamos / con respeto* (in the secret world / we walk / with respect), *no distingo entre labios y raíces* (I do not distin-guish between lips and roots), *no sé, no sé de donde* (I don't know, I don't know whence), *no sabía qué decir, mi boca / no sabía / nombrar* (I did not know what to say, my mouth did not know how to name).

Specification is in order here because the total effect, in *Black Island Memorial*, flickers from point to point like marsh gas, with no expectation of an explosive outcome. It is not given to Neruda, as agonist of the Lost, to shield his eyes in the presence of the mind's transfiguration: neither blinded nor prostrate, he looks steadily into the impurities of duration—animal, vegetal, and mineral,

> while a luster is borne underground, antiquity's
>   princeling
> in his natural grave-clothes of sickening mineral,
> until we are tardily there, too late to be there at all:
> being and not being, life takes its being from these.

Only once is he permitted to see "plainly: one evening, / in India" when, gazing steadily into the flames of a riverside suttee, he sees "something move out of the burning sarcophagus / —call it smoke or a spirit—" and remains until all is consumed, leaving only "night and the water, the dark / and the river, steadfast in that place and that dying." The world's body and the combustion of the world's body: these are the themes of the saint's vigil and man's image of the world's loss.

The point finally to be made, in this uneasy reading of an equivocal legend, is that the *perdido* pursues Neruda throughout the whole compass of his *Memorial*, as a function, rather than a defection, of memory. One could, I am sure, make a tidy case for the first four volumes as the poet's odyssey or hegira through all four elements of the substantive universe— (1) Water (*Donde nace la lluvia: Where the Rain Begins*), (2) Air (*La luna en el laberinto: The Moon in the Labyrinth*), (3) Fire (*El cruel fuego: The Cruel Fire*), and (4) Earth (*El cazador de raices: The Root-Hunter*). Since History and Memory weave themselves equally into his great design, it might be specified for the curious that Water is cognate with the poet's Temucan childhood, Air, with the erotic and the passional, Fire, with revolutionary upheaval and world war, and Earth with the poet's return to his sources on the Chilean mainland: a thoroughly Blakean cosmology. Over this tidy collocation of elements and events, however, as over the burning suttee, moves the Spirit of the Place, surrounded by all the paraphernalia of quantitative optimism, brooding on the Lost, like Dürer's Lady of the Melancholies. If there is any question regarding the persistence of the Lost, one has only to follow the path of the *perdido* into the fifth and final volume, which Neruda somewhat misleadingly has entitled *Sonata crítica* (*Critical Sonata*), as though disengagement and perspective had at last been achieved. Here the tally is no less obliterating than in Book One: Neruda, as card player, "plays for the sake of losing" (*juego / para seguir perdiendo*); he is "lost in the night" (*perdido en la noche*); "there is no longer left [him] a place to lose / the key, the truth, or the lie" (*no hay donde perder / la llave, la verdad, ni la mentira*); we have "all lost the battle" (*todos perdimos la batalla*); "the truth has died" (*ya se murió la verdad*); humanity "loses its way" (*esta humanidad que pierde el rumbo*); the pure being is "lost between words" (*el casto ser perdido entre palabras*); life is "passed or lost" (*cuanta vida / pasamos o perdimos*); memory "trembles in the lost shadow" (*tiembla mi memoria en la sombra perdida*); the "salt is scattered and lost" (*una sal esparcida y perdida*); the wind's sigh remains "lost in the leaves" (*sigue el susurro del viento perdido en las hojas*); but, none the less, "I have found my lost roots" (*encontré mis raices perdidos*).

It would be both mischievous and myopic to suggest on the basis of such passages that *Black Island Memorial* is the labyrinthine complaint of a defeated and despairing man. On the contrary, Neruda's steadfast confrontation of the Lost, his avid immediacies and open-ended determination to live "between the luminous and the desperate halves," measure the strenuous vitalism of his position. It is the Muse of Memory, as Keats' Hyperion was also to discover in the fallen world of Titans, sifting the passing event for its "Names, deeds, gray legends, dire events, rebellions, /

Majesties, sovran voices, agonies, / Creations and destroyings"[28] that "shows the heart's secret to an ancient power" with an intimacy impossible to History. And it is the double vision of the later Neruda, committed equally to Mnemosyne and Clio, that demands an exact accounting from the poet of "what is past, and passing, and to come."[29] Neruda, looking back at his bulking *Memorial*, unfinished to the very end, declares in the *Critical Sonata*: "He who sings both dies and does not die, he who sings goes on living and dying"; he "sings the earthly and heavenly tower from the abyss." It is thus that the *poeta enlutado*, reading the oceans and weathers of Black Island, construing interstices, gaps, collapses, losses, with a passion that dazzles the imagination, holds in his keeping the plenty and certainty of the world. No poet living has braced the whole of his talent on that "point of intersection of the timeless / With time" with a comparable freedom from cant and preconception, or more resolutely approximated the "occupation for a saint."

[1]Alfredo Cardona Peña, *Pablo Neruda y otros ensayos* (Mexico: Ediciones de Andrea, 1955), pg. 40.

[2]See *Visiones de las hijas de Albión y El viajero mental (Visions of the Daughters of Albion and The Mental Traveler) por William Blake* (Madrid: Cruz y Raya, 1934). Also republished by Ediciones Botella Al Mar, undated. His translation of *Romeo and Juliet* has recently been published by Editorial Losada, S.A., Buenos Aires, 1966, as No. 308 in their *Biblioteca clásica y contemporánea*.

[3]"Sobre una poesía sin pureza," *Obras completas (Buenos Aires: Editorial Losada, S.A., 1957)*, pp. 1822-23. Translated in *Selected Poems of Pablo Neruda*, tr. and ed. by Ben Belitt, Introduction by Luis Monguió (New York: Grove Press, 1961), pp. 39-40.

[4]See first edition of *Estravagario* as published by Editorial Losada (Buenos Aires, 1958). The adornments, profuse in the original edition, are omitted in the more recent *Obras completas*, Editorial Losada (1962) (1968).

[5]"Hymne," *Oeuvres complètes* (Paris: Bibliothèque de la Pléiade, Librairie Gallimard, 1954), p. 222.

[6]*Ibid.*, "L'Invitation au Voyage," p. 127.

[7]I: "Proletarian Literature," William Empson, *English Pastoral Poetry* (New York: W. W. Norton and Co., 1938), p. 12.

[8]"Oceanografía dispersa," *Obras completas* (Buenos Aires: Editorial Losada, S.A., 1957), pp. 1825-27.

[9]*Ibid.*, p. 1825: "In this way, the green whale *(Bachianetas glaucus)*, enroute to the South Pacific and the warm islands facing my windows in Isla Negra, gets his nourishment."

[10]*Ibid.*, "Algunas palabras para este libro de piedras," p. 1717. A whimsical allusion to the poems in *The Stones of Chile*.

[11]*Ibid.*, "A Matilde Urrutia," p. 1649. The 'little houses" are, of course, the sonnets of *One Hundred Love Sonnets*.

[12]Work in progress, of which a fragment, entitled *"Amores: Matilde"* appears in Volume V *(Sonata crítica)* of *Memorial de Isla Negra*. Further "fragments" appear in a pamphlet published by Ediciones de la Rama Florida (Lima: 1966), in an edition limited to 300 numbered copies. The volume itself was published in December 1967 by Editorial Losada (Buenos Aires).

[13]Friedrich Nietzsche, *The Birth of Tragedy*, tr. Francis Golffing (Garden City: Doubleday Anchor, 1956), p. 90.

[14]*Selected Poems of Pablo Neruda*, tr. and ed. by Ben Belitt, Introduction by Luis Monguió (New York: Grove Press, 1961), p. 29.

[15]*Ibid.*, pp. 226-233.

[16]Cf. Neruda's *"Los muertos de rostro tierno," "Los más amados muertos,"* with Rilke's *"den jugendlich Toten" (Die Sechste Elegie)* and the dead lovers of *Die Erste Elegie.*

[17]"First Elegy," Rainer Maria Rilke, *Duino Elegies*, tr. Stephen Spender (New York: W. W. Norton, 1939), p. 20.

[18]Sonnet XX, *The Poetical Works of John Keats*, edited by H. W. Garrod (New York, London, Toronto: Oxford University Press, 1956), p. 372.

[19]Neruda's name for his so-called "House in the Sand." The elaborate homage *("La Chascona")* which concludes the *Memorial*, as a whole, however, seems to synthesize two of the poet's houses—"Casa La Chascona" and "Casa La Sebastiana" in the San Cristobal hills overlooking the Santiago harbor and the right bank of the Mapocho River. Both were vandalized—the latter irreparably—after his death. For a picture book of Isla Negra, with photographs by Sergio Larrain and a text in poetry and prose by Pablo Neruda, see *Una casa en la arena (A House in the Sand)* (Barcelona: Editorial Lumen, 1966).

[20]S. T. Coleridge, *Biographia Literaria*, Chapter XIII.

[21]*The Confessions of Saint Augustine*, edited, and with an introduction by Arthur Symons (Walter Scott, Ltd.).

[22]Thus Selden Rodman, in "A Day with Pablo Neruda," *Saturday Review of Literature*, July 9, 1966: "I saw him as a Buddha, ageless, perfectly composed, with just the suggestion of a childlike smile around the corners of his sensual mouth." And in a recent issue of *ABC* (Barcelona), *"Neruda como es,"* Luis María Anson writes: "The poet, converted into a living god, an immutable Dalai Lama, reads an ode, heard with all the intentness of a religious prayer."

[23]Cf. Neruda's *"las cuatro estaciones del alma"* (the four stations of the soul), invoked in the concluding line of *"Cuanto pasa en un día"*: "How Much Happens in a Day."

[24]"The Dry Salvages," T. S. Eliot, *Four Quartets* (New York: Harcourt Brace, 1943), p. 27.

[25]"Infant Sorrow," *Blake's Poetical Works*, edited by John Sampson (London: Oxford University Press, 1938), p. 100.

[26]Reprinted in the *Obras completas*, 1957, pp. 19-30. Translated, with certain omissions, by Ben Belitt, under the title "A Pine Cone, A Toy Sheep . . . " in *Evergreen Review*, Vol. 6, No. 22, Jan.-Feb. 1962, pp. 22-35. Reprinted in *Evergreen Review Reader* (New York: Grove Press, 1968).

[27]Hero and heroine of the piratical *Sandokan* by Emilio Salgari (1863-1911), nostalgically invoked by Neruda in his "Childhood and Poetry."

[28]"Hyperion," *The Poetical Works of John Keats*, edited by H. W. Garrod (New York, London, Toronto: Oxford University Press, 1956), p. 242.

[29]"Sailing to Byzantium," *The Collected Poems of W. B. Yeats* (New York: Macmillan, 1951), p. 192.

10

The Moving Finger and the Unknown Neruda

The moving finger writes,
and having writ, moves on . . .

I.

It has been the fate of moving talents to offer stationary targets to partisan and tendentious readers. Neruda belongs with Protean spirits like Blake ("The cistern contains: the fountain overflows";) and Yeats, who threw his mythological coat to the dogs and chose to "walk naked." Until recently, the erosion of Pablo Neruda has been confined to his South American critics, of friendly and hostile persuasions. Indeed, the attempt of Neruda to keep his vision large in a diminishing world has been one of his constant themes during the last two decades. Between the pedantic and political reductions of his expositors he has interposed an apparatus designed to deflect—at strategic intervals—the Trojan gifts of the "experts." His principal weapons have been three: enigma, caprice, and a Socratic epistemology of "ignorance" which absolutely rejects all vested outcomes, including the dialectical fatalism of the Marxist. As early as 1950, he took pains, in a work of 569 pages devoted for the most part to the historical and geological recovery of a public universe, to infiltrate a poem called "The Enigmas" as a kind of spiritual watermark:

> I am that net waiting emptily—out of range
> of the onlooker, slain in the shadows,
> fingers inured to a triangle, a timid
> half-circle computed in orange.

Probing a starry infinitude
I came like yourselves
through the mesh of my being, in the night,
   and awoke to my nakedness—
all that was left of the catch, a fish
   in the noose of the wind.

With the increasing polarization of his critics, Neruda has had to adopt increasingly Daedalian measures, inventing whole labyrinths, like the unplaceable *Book of Vagaries* (*Extravagario*, 1958), from which there is no rational exit, to outwit his tidiers. In that extraordinary funhouse of metaphysical pratfalls, he has curved all the mirrors with illusions joyously calculated to confront the gullible with parabolic distortions of their own meddlesome intrusions:

I would know nothing, dream nothing:
who will teach my non-being
how to be, without striving to be?

                       ("Estación inmóvil")

or:

I must wait for myself, as they wait for me there:
I also would see myself coming
and know in the end how it feels to me
when I come back to the place where I wait for my coming
and turn back to my sleep, and die laughing.

                                ("Pastoral")

or:

I don't know which way to be—
absent minded or respectful;
shall I yield to advice
or tell them outright they're hysterical?
Independence, it's clear, gets me nowhere.
I get lost in the underbrush,
I don't know if I'm coming or going.
Shall I take off or stand firm,
buy tomatoes or tomcats?

                        ("Partenogénesis")

or finally:

> I'll figure out as best I can
> what I ought *not* to do—and then do it . . .
> if I don't make mistakes
> who'll believe in my errors? . . .
> I'll change my whole person . . .
> and then when I'm different
> and no one can recognize me
> I'll keep doing the same things I did,
> since I couldn't possibly do otherwise.

("Partenogénesis")

Most recently, the Congress of Swedish Academicians (1971) has enlisted a homogenized Neruda: "For poetry that, with the action of an elemental force, brings alive a continent's destiny and dream." The Nobel citation serves to chisel into the steles of posterity, like a Roman grave marker, the curious longing of Neruda's idolators: the wish for a stationary god, a known rather than an unknown god, a tractable god whose sources go docilely back to Whitman or Darío or Karl Marx—a fixed eminence pointing one way, like the profiles of Easter Island, toward the Chilean mainland: a mausoleum, a patriotic rubric for the good life, an irreversible Position. Precisely this is the measure of the anguish of Neruda's contradictory venture: to keep "empty," to test the commitments of a lifetime with imaginative acts of "non-being" forcing the poet to pit the personal against the political life; to invite trial by negation, reversal, suspension, self-doubt, in a hazardous insistence upon muddlement: to be "rector of nothing" (*rector de nada*).

There is hardly any need, I think, to labor the obvious and painful conversion of Neruda by his Latin-American admirers into a national acropolis and a gun emplacement for an ideological invasion. Nothing less elevated than the heights of Macchu Picchu will do. Neruda has recently protested in prose to a number of reporters whose questions were baited for more conventional outcomes. To *Le Monde*'s interviewer,[1] primarily concerned with the theme of multiple identities in *Extravagario*, he remarked: "When I was an exclusively introverted poet I was accused of being nonpolitical. Then when I spoke out in behalf of man and man's suffering I was dragged off by the ears like a schoolboy and reprimanded by others. They have turned me into a shooting gallery." To an audience at the University of Chile he confided:[2]

The poet is not a "little god"; he has not stolen celestial fire; he is not the offspring of a special race, androgynous or malign. He is a craftsman with a function. His function is no more important than other functions, except when he dares to confront the forces of social reaction. And that is dangerous too, because the poet speaks as a custodian of the truth.

He went on to elaborate to his Parisian interviewer:

> Every one of my poems is a little like a leap into the blue; I alternately jump out of the window onto the street, and back again through the window off of the street. I have always rejected a positional poetry (*poesía de especialista*) and shall always refuse to enclose myself in a single poetic modality (*un solo género poético*). After *Canto general*, it seemed to me I had exhausted the geo-historical concept of a poetry essentially preoccupied with the Latin-American continent and ambience. Afterwards, I was threatened on all sides by purely pathetic incursions. I had to find a different tone, I had to *learn how to play* (*aprender a jugar*). I abandoned a terrorist or sanguinary poetry to write edible verses, verses like treacle. I was straightway accused of being a programmatic optimist. I have never renounced my right to express the loneliness, the anguish, or the horror of things. My job is to capture the sounds, mingle the colors, probe for the vital power of things wherever they are to be found, by due process of creation and destruction.

Nevertheless, the myopic proscription of Neruda has gone on, and has recently been imported into this country by anthologists and translators, by a kind of reverse imperialism which seeks to immobilize his diversity in "simplified" versions for the common reader. Robert Bly, for example, for all his raucous devotion to the genius of Neruda, has not only annexed him to the American Middle West, but finally bound him back-to-back with César Vallejo in a maudlin formula for the "open" way in poetry. Neruda took pains to point out the misdirection in an interview[3] with Mr. Bly, after courteously acknowledging his good intentions:

> "I like very much the way you approach us—that you bring us near each other in our work worlds. I never thought of it . . . Nevertheless, we were very different. Race especially. He was Peruvian. He was a very Peruvian man—" [by which, Neruda went on to specify, he meant that Vallejo was Indian.] "I don't have it," he concluded categorically. "I am a Castilian poet. In Chile we defend the Indians and almost all South Americans have some Indian blood, I do too. But I don't think my work is in any way Indian."

Typical of the programmatic reduction of Neruda by Mr. Bly is the bristling choice of a title for his Introduction to an anthology, *Twenty Poems*, loosely distributed over a period of twenty-nine years: "Refusing To be Theocritus." The phrase itself, excerpted from a diffuse and journalistic poem to the Venezuelan poet, Miguel Otero Silva, in effect equates the total accomplishment of Neruda with an episode in the '40s convenient for the purposes of Mr. Bly. His implied derogation of the pastoral way has a ring of evangelical ferocity. Theocritus, apparently, belongs with Watteau and Marie Antoinette—a perpetual fancy-dress ball in which shepherdesses converse with shepherds twelve months of the year about love and scenery, and nothing ever changes but the seasons. In place of Theocritus, Bly has chosen to elevate an urban, unmetaphysical Neruda confronting the Secret Police of González Videla "with hands stained with depression and garbage"—and hold him to that tableau throughout the *Residencia en la tierra* (1925-1945), *Canto general* (1950), and the *Odas elementales* (1954-1959) like a panel in a post-office mural.

That is the *known* Neruda: the public klaxon or forensic convenience to which all roads have led with a shocking paucity of exceptions. Where exceptions exist, they have been the result of open-ended reading by inductive observers whose concern is with the momentum and idiosyncracies of a total vision incorruptibly committed to its impulses. Thus it is that Neruda's discerning bibliographer at the University of Chile chose the motif of "Being and Dying"[4] as the riddle of the "moving finger" of Pablo Neruda; and the poet's Uruguayan biographer, in a more subtle reversal of that paradox, has traced the itinerary of an "Immobile Traveler".[5] The Neruda of both Hernán Loyola and Emir Rodríguez Monegal is seen not only face-fo-face, but face after face. Each follows the contradictory voyage of a poet in its Lilliputian and Brobdingnagian phases, without regard for equations of size or the protocol of the heroic stance. And, in fairness to Bly, it must be pointed out that even he sees somewhere in the middle distance a Neruda who "contains an astonishing variety of earthy things that swim in a sort of murky water," while opting for a "surrealist" activist.

And Neruda—what has he seen? Neruda's mistrust of his mentors— those presumably in the know, feeding an epoch's computers with cue cards for the mating of a poet with the politically nubile and lonely—has alternately plagued and amused him. His form of saying so has been odic —Theocritan:

Came the critics: one deaf
and one gifted with tongues,
and others and others:
the blind and the hundred-eyed,
the elegant ones
in red pumps and carnations,
others decently clad
like cadavers . . .
some coiled in the forehead
of Marx or thrashing about in his whiskers;
others were English,
just English . . .

("Oda a la crítica")

In 1968 he was both truculent and fey:

They keep after me
with their questions: what are my relations
with cats, how I discovered the rainbow,
why the worth of the chestnut
is contained in its burr . . .
they want, of all things to know
the bull-frog's opinion: what do
the animals under their burrows
in the fragrance of forests or
in pustules of asphalt, make of my life?

("Abejas I")

With a marksman's eye for advancing guards and the changing of vogues, he recently remarked to a startled reporter in Buenos Aires[6] (on a mission from the erudite *Razón y fábula* of Colombia's Universidad de los Andes):

I assume that in a country (like Chile) that is going Socialist, the direction of poetry would have to be one of diversification, and that every poet would leave his own mark on the changing tradition. There must always be this diversity: that, precisely, is what insures the flowering of poetry under any circumstance. It's impossible to specify any one single road, poetry has many ways, every conceivable way . . . Poetry is always changing . . . In Chile (the Chile of Allende) poets have no intention of writing in any but their accustomed manner . . . We are about to nationalize a publishing house to serve the Chilean Republic—a colossal undertaking which has both its advantages and its possible risks.

Prodded by his questioner about "the future of poetry in a technological world", his reply was nothing less than ambassadorial:

> The jets breaking the sound barrier, and similar noises known to us all are altering the silence of the world. Poets are free to participate or not in the great hubbub of human progress on a technological level proper to such matters; but they must always keep sacrosanct some recess dedicated to their spiritual intimacy, to the task of self-knowledge, to the eternal experiment with words, sounds, and dreams. For my own part, I have been influenced by all sorts of things in the exterior world, but I insist that nothing in the world that pressures us all with its gravity lessen my intimacy with myself. There's a verse of Whitman's that says: "Nothing exterior will ever command me completely."

Moving in closer, Neruda has constantly triangulated the stresses ("I remain steadfastly triangular") and jousted with faulting tastes and reputations in the aftermath of political eruptions. On occasion, would-be supplanters like Nicanor Parra have been named for him; at other times he has known where to plant the banderillas himself: Juan Larrea, or a whole *cuadrilla* of university *vallejistas* determined to undermine his prestige by the expropriation of a talent whose angle of vision has been repeatedly eulogized by Neruda in prose, verse, and personal interview: Peru's César Vallejo. Only two years ago, Neruda observed with characteristic taciturnity:

> Those who were lately nerudarized
> (*Todos los que nerudearon*)
> are beginning to vallejolate
> (*comenzaron a vallejarse*)
> and before that cock crowed
> they settled for Eliot or Perse
> and drowned in their fishpond.
>
> Nevertheless, I go on spinning
> my own ancestral time-table,
> chintzier with each passing day
> without discovering so much as a flower
> not already discovered by others,
> or inventing a single
> fixed star not already extinct.
>
> ("Ayer")

While others have been firing up their boilers for midnight runs to the border, Neruda has contemptuously rejected all schedules and itineraries of the *avant-garde*, including their technological fixation on a "new" poetry for all. Even his imagery has been tatterdemalion, quixotic, old hat.

> Next time I come back
> into time astride my habitual nag
> I'll give all my attention to stalking
> anything that moves—in the sky, on the ground,
> with the regulation hunterly crouch:
> that way, ahead of the game, I can check
> on what is or isn't invented already,
> discovered, or still undiscovered.
>
> ("Ayer")

For Neruda in 1972, the rather seedy and categorical mésalliance of all Latin American modernism with Walt Whitman is still good enough, though he continued to press for the "Castilian" refinements of Góngora and Quevedo. His lapidary essay on Quevedo (*circa* 1936) deserves to be better known, as well as the sumptuous Gongorism of certain sonnets and barcaroles, and those baroque infiltrations (called "surrealist") that reverse the plodding journalism of lyric after lyric with seventeenth-century extravagances:

> Distance feeds on my clothing
> as I climb the titanic perspectives
>
> ("Volver volviendo")

or a seascape:

> Convulsions, the tortoise's bitterness,
> a murderer's panoply.
> diapasons, wars to the death,
> a piano of slaughterer's teeth
>
> ("Marejada en 1968: Océano Pacífico")

or the polarization of a crystal:

the diamond's linear water: the maze
in the sapphire and its gothic magnificence:
the multiplication of rectangles
in the nut of the amethyst . . .
the salt's school; the decorum of fire.

("El cuadrado al cristal")

To this day, devotees of "Macchu Picchu" tend to forget that Section IX of that poem combines a Communist's metaphysics of rational faith with a counterplay of images which might tax the fantasy of a Gongorist, and merits Fernando Alegría's epithet of "churrigueresco."

Even the *poetas celestes*, the introspective pantheon of Rilke, Kafka, and Gide formerly denounced by Neruda as "obscurantists, false/existential witch doctors, surrealist/butterflies ablaze/on the carrion," have been recently assimilated into his oceanic tolerance as another part of the imaginative field. If Neruda is no longer a Theocritan, he is plainly Ovidian in his metamorphic passion for *change* as a mode of virility and a dynamic of cosmological love. He has changed not only from fat poems to skinny ones, or from open poems to orphic utterance; he has periodically changed the whole currency of his thinking—the mind of a man, as well as the mind of a poet—in a lifelong ventilation of commitments. Asked for his views regarding "the celestial poets" in 1966,[7] he replied disarmingly: "I must say I have been mistaken many times in my life. I was dogmatic and foolish . . . Excuse me, but the contradictions—one sees them only when life rolls on, one sees one has been mistaken. Kafka is a great writer." And more recently, Borges, who has not yet returned the compliment with comparable gusto, is "not only a great Argentine writer, but one of the most important in the entire world."[8] Rimbaud, Emerson, Schiller, de Vigny, Hugo, Mallarmé, Apollinaire—the vegetal and the cerebral poets alike—have all been acknowledged as republican spirits in a tentative venture in which poets of all persuasions are indisolubly allied. "Who's to say whether one or the other approaches to poetry is the permanently viable one"?[9] This has not prevented him from changing his mind again in 1969 in another sweeping derogation of Verlaine, the "umbrellas of Baudelaire," the combined encumbrances of Balzac ("an elephant"), Hugo ("a truck"), Tolstoi ("a mountain"), Zola ("a cow"), and Mallarmé again ("a pastry-cook"), in favor of "Uncle Ubu Dada," who had the wit to say *merde* to them all.

Similarly, Neruda's revision of set-pieces variously entitled "The Poet," "Arte poética," or "Artés poéticas," over the years has been especially instructive and diverting, and continues into *World's End* (*Fin de mundo*, 1969) with two further variations on the theme. In *Residencia I* (1925-1931), for example, his inflection was one of plangent and harrowing melancholy, "between dark and the void . . . with my singular heart and my mournful conceits for my portion," and his poetics, a grinding ordeal of existential "absence" poised for a breakthrough which only the disaster of the Spanish Civil War could disclose to him:

> For every invisible drop that I taste in a stupor, alas,
> for each intonation I concentrate, shuddering,
> I keep the identical thrust of an absence, the identical
> chill of a fever . . .
> Could it be differently put, a little less ruefully, possibly?—
> All the truth blurted out?
>
> ("Arte poética")

In the end, he yielded to the pathos of the deracinated predicament and produced two other *Residencias* (1931-1935), (1935-1945) in an

> impact of objects that call and encounter no answer,
> unrest without respite, the anomalous mind
>
> ("Arte poética")

In *Canto general* (1950) the tone was more militant, though still obsessively retrospective in its bid for a larger vision hostile to the death-will and the limited life:

> That time when I moved among happenings
> in the midst of my mournful devotions . . .
> the inhuman contention of masks and existences. I
> endured in the bog-dweller's element . . .
> Estranged to myself, like shadow on water
> I sped through the exile of each man's existence
> this way and that, and so, to habitual loathing.
>
> ("El poeta")

Here the conclusion may be called diagnostic or homeopathic: the physician, having learned how to heal himself, offers his pharmacopeia to all:

> I saw that their being was this: to stifle
> one half of existence's fulness like fish
> in an alien margin of ocean.

("El poeta")

By contrast, the poetics of *World's End* (1969) seem almost oafishly insouciant, unbuttoned, unforensic: a poetics of vagary rather than the hard line of programmatic self-criticism:

> All really superior poets
> laugh at my penmanship—
> because of the punctuation—
> while I keep thumping my breast
> confessing my commas and periods,
> colons, exclamation points:
> all the incestuous and criminal
> acts that have buried my words
> in a Dark Ages special to me,
> like provincial cathedrals.

("Ayer")

Of his two recent "Artes poéticas," the first, folksy and cerebral by turns, maintains a tone of garrulity and avoids the nomenclature common to the esthetics of the imaginative process. Neruda puts on hat over hat over hat, with a clown's disregard for the gravity of alternative functions. He is carpenter-poet, "cutting into the board / of my choice / with the sputtering point of my saw"; a baker "wading in, to my elbows, / kneading the glare of the oven / into watery green language" /; and "blacksmith, perhaps," who requires "of myself and my verses . . . a metallurgical medium." His conclusion is to shrug off conclusion ("One poet's experience / with manual metaphysics / doesn't make a poetics"):

> In this free confraternity
> I've no burning allegiances.
> I was always a lone iron-monger.

"Artes Poéticas (II)" is even more spindly and wayward in its total disregard for the premise of visionary Romanticism—the Rimbaldian *voyant* or the Baudelairean *voyageur* pointing his prow toward infinity with a satanic insistence on the abyss of the Unexperienced, *"Enfer ou Ciel, qu'importe?"* For Neruda, the point for poetry is precisely the opposite: the enigmatic is what is totally given us, what is totally *there*—inexhaustible, ordinary, inapprehensible:

> I've discovered nothing at all;
> all was already discovered
> when I ambled into the world.
> If I come back this way
> I entreat all discoverers
> to leave something for me—
> some unnamed volcano,
> the secret source of a river,
> an anonymous madrigal.

II

The point for the poetry of Pablo Neruda could also be a wholly disastrous one. There will always be those who rise to remark that I have been inadvertently notarizing the bankruptcy and not the enrichment of a talent: that this is a cave-in, a sell-out, the creeping liquidation of both a poet and a political conscience. The "unknown Neruda" by this right would be an eccentric and obsolescent Neruda—anti-intellectual, chaplinesque, incorrigible: a poet without contour, rigor, or direction. Such a mischievous reading of the record would confirm again the old longing for a monolithic Neruda, or the mandate for a permanent one—both inadmissible procedures in the critical appraisal of poets of genius anywhere in the world.

That I have been noting an anti-heroical trend in the posture of the later Neruda, however, is a reading I would happily affirm. The "unknown Neruda" must first be transposed from the heights of Macchu Picchu—which, after all, is borrowed *tierra* of distinctly Indian antiquity —to Isla Negra, which has served for years as the bastion of a troubled Chilean turning his vision outward and inward to answer the enigma of the displaced identity in a "century of the stateless man": "What can I do without roots?" The great poem of the "unknown Neruda" is not "Las alturas de Macchu Picchu" but "Fin de fiesta" ("Party's End") from the *Cantos ceremoniales* (1961)—a poem of haunting equivocations, with an "island music" as subtle as the watery and earthy noises caught in mid-air by the drunkards of *The Tempest*. As steward and enchanter of that island, Neruda, with wand and book, evokes the innocence of a "brave new world that hath such people in it," visions of shipwreck, dispossession, and the corrupt polity of the old world, while preparing a sea-change for a stranger reassertion of reality. For his attendant sprites he has both Ariel and Caliban; and behind them, the darker mythopoeia of Sycorax, the island's ambiguous progenetrix: daimons of earth, air, water, and fire, a supplanted and vaguely apotheosized mother, a "brusque father" buried "in one of the rainiest graveyards of the world," an enigma directed variously at the human dream of liberty and the geology of the cosmos. All is in readiness, it would seem, for a Theocritan return to an idyl in the twentieth-century style—the metropolitan pastoral of a good society in which worker talks to worker twelve months of the year about love and the economics of abundance and nothing ever changes but the seasons.

It is precisely here, however, that the "unknown Neruda" intervenes, with a shocking reversal of protocol. What is likely to puzzle and mortify the partisan reader of *World's End* most is the unsparing embitterment of Neruda's castigation of a century, thirty years in advance of its legal and historical demise. Hernán Loyola[10] tells us that *Fin de mundo* originally bore the title of *Juicio final* (*Last Judgment*)—a wholly different conception from the kind of periodic stock-taking to which Neruda has shown an abiding partiality—last testaments, autumnal testaments, testimonials, witnesses, in the spirit of François Villon: "I am the sonorous man / witness (*testigo*) to the hopes of this murderous century." An overlay of all these titles—*Fin de fiesta, Fin de mundo, Juico final*—reveals the eschatological passion with which Neruda, writing as though every book was his last, since *Canto general*, and signing his vision of judgment with his flayed skin, like Michelangelo, has finally aggrandized his dream of the human condition.

> I wait at this door
> for those still to come to this party's end:
> to this end of the world.
>
> ("La puerta")

The roll call of despairing epithets applied to his century in *World's End* is literally annihilating: one would have to go back to Jeremiah or to *The Wasteland* to equal it. "This is the hollow century," "This is the epoch of ashes," "This is the century of agony / that taught us how to kill / and to dislike survivors," "This century swarming / with rightists and leftists / robbers of man, usurpers / kidnappers, murderers," the "electronic century" of a "new god with an eye in its forehead / to kill us," "the century of the displaced man / the book of displacement / the dark century, the black book / given me to write and hold to the light." Indeed, it would seem that Neruda's "book of displacement" is even more lethal than he may have bargained for: Timon of Athens has moved into the island kingdom of Prospero and reigns as tyrant of a malevolent century:

> We hear not only the knife
> cutting the sky
> and dividing the planets,
> but in damnable islands the poets
> of Athens still live in chains.
>
> ("Siglo")

> The truth is: I never understood
> anyone's messages . . .
> Only the Ocean existed.
>
> ("El mar")

> I have lived one hundred years
> moving from one war to the next
> drinking blood out of books,
> out of newspapers and
> television, at home
> on trains, in the Spring,
> in my mourning for Spain.
>
> ("Vivir cien años")

> The truth is that there is no truth.
>
> ("Exilios")

This, too, is an unknown Neruda—the most misanthropic given us since his purgatorial voyage through three *Residencias*—a Neruda to be reckoned with, as one reckons with the contrary states of innocence and experience of the "Mental Traveler" (a poem translated by Neruda in 1935) in Blake's similar search for revolutionary "progression." For revolution and progression are *there*: they are the inalienable act of faith in a long discipline of *"deberes"*—the heart as well as the conscience of Neruda's poetics of "obligation." What has apparently withered away is the dialectical optimism of a Marxist reading of history. While others have turned to "the hypothetical politician / who leads without leadership / invisible multitudes," Neruda has remained a "lone iron-monger"—a type of the simultaneous man ordering the chaos of poetry by spontaneous enactments of being, rather than a time-table for the withering away of the dictator-ship by the proletariat. As of 1972, *all* is equally "impure" for Neruda: poetry, history, destiny, the hope of the world, while a poet who has "learned how to *play*" with fatality as well as envision and indict it, "plays with the darkness / without forgetting the good days."

It is in "games" as vast and portentous as this that the tensions of "The Hands of Day," "World's End," and "Skystones" (*Piedras del cielo*: 1970) must be realigned to engage the full magnitude of the unknown Neruda. The "games" are the games which poets of multinational genius have always played, to the exasperation of philosopher kings and theoret-ical utopists: the games by which we recognize the truly laureate poet, who comes to say in the end that "Hamlet and Lear are gay." It is not idle perversity that induces Neruda to write in the twilight of an obsessional "song of myself":

> Condemned to self-love
> I lived the exterior life of a hypocrite
> hiding the depths of the love
> my defects brought down on my head.
> I keep on being happy,
> disclosing to nobody
> my ambiguous malady:
> the grief I endure for self-love,
> who was never so loved in return.

> ("Condiciones")

and to add:

> The harsher the street sounds became,
> the sweeter I seemed to myself.

The "happiness" of Neruda is apparent throughout each of the three volumes excerpted for this collection: it is the "ounce of civet" with which an offended imagination has been sweetened in antic and diminished acts of lyricism. The tone is not euphoric or rational, but vitalistic and dis-engaged; and the sweetness is the sweetness of a whole organism soundly fulfilling its visceral and intellectual life functions. Neruda is neither eclectic, nor ambivalent, nor contradictory in the sense that one has reason to anticipate a synthesis that never materializes: he is merely as multiple as he needs to be. There is room even for Theocritus: he returns as "root-hunter" (*cazador de raíces*) and interpreter of rains and volcanoes in the *Memorial de Isla Negra* (1964), writing landscape after landscape, attempting a paganization of the myth of Genesis in *The Burning Sword* (*La espada encendida*: 1970), and finally turning the Pacific itself into a pasture of plankton for the grazing of narwhals and leviathans. The uncanny light of that serenity is the mark of the "unknown Neruda" as the light of Velásquez is the signature of the later Velásquez. It shows us Neruda at his games and *deberes*, indicting a century, "playing" with the cyclical notion of a century of "hands" (more "manual metaphysics!") in "The Hands of Day," and transmuting the *Stones of Chile* (*Las piedras de Chile*: 1961)—the rocky crenelations of his island fortress of Isla Negra— into geological transparencies. In 1970, whatever is hardest, least diaphanous and destructible, most geometrical in the vision of Pablo Neruda has turned into a crystal fitting for the divinations of a sibyl: "the stones of the sky."

[1]Aline Schulmann (trans)., "La única ley del arte es vida", *Clarín literario* (Buenos Aires, October 28, 1971).
[2]Uboldo Nicchi, "La vida en versos", *Clarín literario*.
[3]Pablo Neruda, *Twenty Poems* (Madison, Minn., The Sixties Press, 1967). Translated by James Wright and Robert Bly, with Introduction and Interview by Robert Bly.
[4]Hernán Loyola, *Ser y morir en Pablo Neruda* (Santiago, Editorial Santiago, 1967).
[5]Emir Rodríguez Monegal, El viajero inmóvil, *Introducción a Pablo Neruda* (Buenos Aires, Editorial Losada, 1966).
[6]Antonio Requieri, "Pablo Neruda en Buenos Aires", *Razón y fábula*, no. 24 (marzo-abril 1971).
[7]*Twenty Poems*, Bly interview.
[8]Requieri, "Pablo Neruda en Buenos Aires".
[9]*Ibid.*
[10]Pablo Neruda, *Antología esencial*, Selección y prólogo de Hernán Loyola (Buenos Aires, Editorial Losada, 1971).

V

Revaluations:

Pablo Neruda—The Man

Nothing has been terminated.
All is yet to come.

11

Neruda's *Memoirs*: * A Reading From Homer

One of the bequests of Walt Whitman to his American *"élèves"*
is an economy of conspicuous redundance. The solipsistic theme
which divinizes the Self and enlists the "cosmical artist-mind lit with the
Infinite" to "confront his manifold and oceanic qualities," is nothing if
not repetitious. In the case of Whitman, it led to the loose-leaf dynamics
of an infinitely expandable work-in-progress into which the divagations of
the Self are made to debouch, as a single exercise in extension. There, the
repetitions of the "Me in the center" seem inseparable from a "quality of
Being, in the object's self, according to its own central idea and purpose,
and of growing therefrom and thereto," like a "lesson in Nature." In the
case of Neruda, committed to "the positive hero" of "the North American
Walt Whitman and the Soviet Mayakovsky," the Song of Myself has
seemed fragmented, ancillary, disparate—an improvisation in search of
its center, whose effect has been tentative and narcissistic, rather than
"postive."

Readers of Neruda are already well acquainted with his autobiographical repertory. They have seen it in its purely erotic guise in the "despairing" singer of his *Twenty Love Poems and a Desperate Song* (1923). It
emerges again in the epilog to his compendious *Canto general*, as "*Yo Soy:
I am*," a geo-political blend of both Villon and Whitman, starting from
the rain-forests of Temuco, as Whitman started from Paumanok, sketch-
ing in his "residence" in the Far East, Mexico, Spain, and his exile from
Chile, and concluding with last wills and testaments to his party and his
tierra (1950). Thereafter, it deviates into autobiographical and occasional
prose, much as Whitman accumulated the entries for his *Specimen Days*:
scattered pages on oceanography, conchology, bottles and figureheads,
gastronomy, Quevedo, the artifacts and gewgaws of Isla Negra, and one

*Memoirs by Pablo Neruda. Translated by Hardie St. Martin. Farrar, Straus & Giroux, New York,
1977.

highly stylized essay of some length on "Childhood and Poetry," which launches Chapter I of the present *Memoirs*. As a serialized autobiography in ten chapters published between March and June (1962) by the Brazilian *revista, O Cruzeiro Internacional*, it resumes the pageants of the Self with the epoch of the *Residencias* and concludes in a Byronic epiphany of exile, studded with nostalgias, the capitals of Europe, and the orders and salutations of the Iron Curtain countries, as "Lives of a Poet" (*"Las vidas del poeta."*) Two years later, on the occasion of his 60th birthday, the Song of Myself reappears in the guise of yet another autobiography in verse, entitled *Memorial de Isla Negra (Black Island Memorial)*, symbiotically scattering the "lives of the poet" throughout five volumes devoted to the fortunes of Neruda and the peninsular bastion which he claimed as his meditative domain in 1939.

The volume of posthumous *Memoirs* draws upon all these antecedent "lives," "memorials," epilogs, "songs", and miscellaneous *hors d'oeuvres*. Refining and expanding in some cases, dilating, compressing, re-aligning in others, hurtling over the riches and disasters of a final decade in an effort to overtake what history and cancer compelled him to foreshorten, the *Memoirs* concludes with "some quick lines only three days after the unspeakable events took my great comrade, Allende, to his death." The title chosen by Neruda for his valedictory volume is no longer "The Lives of a Poet," but the unlovely and ominous declaration: "I Confess I Have Lived," which his American publishers, for reasons of linguistic incompatibility or the search for an elegance absent in the original, have encircled—in Spanish—in the "o" of *Memoirs*, like a mandala. Yet Neruda's true signature for his autobiography, after years of reflection and the addition of some 150 pages, is bound to bemuse those in search of his total legend as a personal historian.

What is the meaning of this confessional posture? Why the past perfect of the verb "to live," rather than the plural of the noun, "lives"? The question is an important one, in so far as it casts new light on a terminal Song of Myself conceived in the twilight of a failed polity and the shadow of physical disaster. "Confession" is a word with either a forensic or a eucharistic ring: in a court of ecclesiastical or secular law, it stands for a public acknowledgment of guilt, and in its religious sense it constitutes a sacramental bid for absolution. Thorny and gauche though it may be to English translation, the confessional posture is the last of Neruda's musical signatures—defiant, ironic, unrelentingly heretical: a vitalist's profession of faith in the life-force which acknowledges only the sanctity of existence and "confesses" nothing but the integrity of its on-going *élan*. Neruda recants nothing, regrets nothing, extenuates nothing, trims nothing. His translation of the pietist's "I confess that I have *sinned*" into the revolutionary's "I confess that I have *lived*" is, in the loftiest Spanish sense, quixotic and parodistic. It calls to mind the premise of yet another of his admired precursors who sought to marry Hell and Heaven in the enigma of a "mental traveler" at large in a "dangerous world" of innocence and experience where "all Act is Virtue."

It would be easy to write all this off as the brag of a militant egoist. Readers of the *Memoirs*, however, moved by the Life in a way that they have not been by the previous personae of his oeuvre, will welcome it as a clue to that "poetics of amplitude" which is the special provenance of the epic. For despite all its shortcomings as a "confession" in the grand manner of the saints or the updated style of the clinically bedevilled, the sheer majesty of the Life comes through with a dazzle that deserves to be called charismatic. Behind the dropping of names, cities, continents, oceans, and cataclysms, the inexhaustible derring-do of geological displacement, one is haunted by a *déjà-vu* which piques the attention. Somewhere, one has met this combination of vastitude, geographical mobility, and fatality before. Neruda is right to caution his readers that "what the memoir writer remembers is not the same thing the poet remembers. He may have lived less, but he photographed more and he re-creates for us with special attention to detail. The poet gives us a gallery full of ghosts shaken by the fire and darkness of his time. Perhaps I didn't live just in myself, perhaps I lived the lives of others." The quick of the matter is touched when Neruda goes on to remark, "From what I have left in writing on these pages will always fall . . . yellow leaves on their way to death and grapes that will find new life in the sacred wine."

It is then that one says: "But the word for the life is—*Homeric!*"

II

I do not mean to suggest by this any comparison, substantive or hermeneutical, of the *Memoirs* of Pablo Neruda with the *Odyssey* of Homer. What I mean to suggest is that the *stature* of Neruda in awesome ways already known to readers of his *Residences*, his *General Song*, his *Black Island Memorial*, and his *Odes*, is everywhere implicit in the "photographic" particulars of his "lives." If there are latter-day Homers, as there are latter-day prophets, then the *Memoirs* of Pablo Neruda comprises a lower-case odyssey that discloses a dimension of the modern imagination measurable up to now only in a succession of "failed epics": a "shoring up of fragments," ruins, Bridges, Cantos, and American Selves already written into the North American canon of our century.

For the effect of the *Memoirs*, without seeking to be so, is over-size, grandiose, *fabulous*. It helps us to understand how the late purveyors of myth come by their magical commodity when the matrix of a new "enlightenment" provides no confirming canons of sanctity—encompassing personalities, transcending history, and writing their vision *large*. It undertakes the re-invention of Homer not as an anachronistic exercise in scale, as Joyce might be said to do, but as the unconscious recapitulation of a great phylum committed to the dynamics of "eternal return." It makes clear that the oeuvre of Pablo Neruda, for all his fondness for the "positive hero" of Whitman and Mayakovsky, was never merely a "song of myself" written for the "Me in the center," but a search for his species.

If, as would also appear, Neruda's "true Penelope" was Chile, he wove and rewove a fabric that was epical rather than personal or patriotic. Least of all can it be said that "politics" was the exclusive or principal concern of the Neruda of the *Memoirs*. As the last of many ostensible "songs of myself" in the teeming plenty of his oeuvre, his autobiography is equally concerned with enigmas, mysteries, ethnic and global wars, demi-gods, captains, kings, cosmological and zoological fantasies, as well as the old Homeric staples: Eros, Mars, and Themis, who presides over the destiny and justice of things. I should like to undertake in the remainder of this essay—whimsically or tediously as the occasion may require—a reading of the *Memoirs* in the "Homeric" mode. My concern, as I hope to make clear, is nothing so jejune as the transformation of an Iliad into a Chiliad; but with the persistence of Homeric staples—Eros, Mars, and Themis—and their aggrandizing force in the evocation of "noble" utterance. What is at issue, to borrow the nomenclature of Wallace Stevens, is "the noble rider and the sound of words."

Readers coming to the prose Life after the Complete Works of the poet need not be reminded that the letter of Pablo Neruda anticipates the Life in its pervasive mingling of both the crepuscular and the erotic themes. They are aware of a twilight melancholy, with its hispanic mask of *soledad* and its gravid professions of sensuous and indefinable despair that drenches Neruda's first phase as a poet of landscapes and *amores*. The results, inconsequential in *Crepusculario* (*Book of Twilight*) (1923), were sufficient in his *20 Love Poems and a Desperate Song* (1924) to launch his reputation as a poet just entering his 20's and assure a circulation of more than a million copies by the time he was 57. In 1952 there were more passionate avowals under the title of *Los versos del capitán*, (*The Captain's Verses*), published anonymously to maintain the poet's double allegiance to a wife and a mistress. By 1953 he was able to provide a whole anthology of Ovidian metamorphoses under the title of *Todo el amor* (*Total Love*). In 1960 he added a century of sonnets to his third wife, Matilde Urrutia, entitled *Cien sonetos de amor* (*100 Love Sonnets*), and in 1967, a cycle of "barcaroles" in which uxorious adulation and a sequence of sea-chanteys were similarly intended as epithalamia for the pleasure of his lady.

The provenance of Eros in the works of Pablo Neruda is, then, at least as consuming and diverse as it is in the *Odyssey*; but its persistence into the Life of the *Memoirs* is no less "Homeric." There comes to mind, in the first third of his chronicle, the anonymous thresher in the haylofts of Hernandez; the menstrual Marisol-and-Marisombra of the *20 Love Poems*; the stranger from the *boîtes* of Les Halles who "got into my bed sleepily and obligingly" to preside over the erotic mysteries and conduct the poet "to the very origins of pleasure"; Josie Bliss, the "Burmese pantheress" whose "jealous tantrums turned into an illness" that threatened the life of the poet, taxed all his sexual prowess as an American sensualist, and provoked his most acerb and exacerbated masterpieces, the *"Tango del viudo"* (*Widow's Tango*) and *"Las furias y las penas"* (*The Woes and the Furies*); Patsy, with her cadre of Boer, English, and Dravidian "girls of various colorings" who "went to bed with me sportingly and asked nothing in return"; the Ceylonese pariah who balanced great buckets of excrement on her head like a matutinal goddess of the privy, and submitted to the solicitations of her clients "with eyes wide open, completely unresponsive"; Kruzi, the Jewess "who had been given a choice between a maharajah, a prince, and a wealthy Chinese merchant" with a trunkful of panties, and was intercepted at the door of her Rolls Royce by the Dutch authorities who "considered it a grave offense for her to live as a concubine of a Chinese."

All serve, in any "epical" reading of the Life, as permutations of Eros, like that triptych of enchantresses whom Homer immortalized in his quadrant of *"belles dames sans merci,"* as if to give visceral and numinous force to the vitalism of his protagonist before returning him to his web-weaving spouse. All elicit avid episodes to themselves in Neruda, as in Homer. Here, in effect, Calypso, "that lady of the lovely locks," "singing in a beautiful voice," moves again in an ambience of caverns, *"birds of the coast whose daily business takes them down to the sea"; Nausicaa flicks a "glistening whip" over her wagon-load of ambrosial laundry on a sea-coast in Phaeacia, enroute to her rendezvous with the naked Odysseus; Circe of the floating islands "singing in her beautiful voice as she went to and fro at her great and everlasting loom" prepares her philtres of "yellow honey flavoured with Pramnian wine," and, at the entrance to the twin whirlpools here also wait those deadliest singers of all, "the Sirens who bewitch everybody that approaches them." As archetypes of erotic enchantment each serves to launch the Odyssey of Homer's much displaced campaigner precisely as the assorted hookers and odalisques of the Orient launch the long exile of Neruda in a picaresque chronicle of deracination, perfidy, and legitimate restorations that mingle the sacred with the sensual and the martial with the political.

III

It is not surprising, therefore, that Neruda's chronicle of Levantine "solitude" should end in a paradox which was to polarize his allegiances as a poet throughout the remainder of a crowded and contradictory career: the affirmation of "mystery," and the irreversible commitment to a militant and quotidian world of man's bread and man's labor. Specifically, it is a *musical* factor that Neruda extrapolates at the conclusion of the first third of his autobiography to epitomize that "secret" ingredient which, in his opinion, had hitherto eluded "the critics who have scrutinized my work":

> Although my poetry is not "fragrant or aerial," (he writes) "but sadly earthbound, I think those qualities, so often clad in mourning, have something to do with my deep feelings for this music that lived within me.

It is that "music," at once daily and alien, heard, at one point in a Cambodian jungle when Neruda "for a terrible moment" believed himself transported "to the spot where I should die" and left to "the fury of my killers" by strangers, and at another, in the casbahs of Colombo, where he stopped his rickshaw while

---

*All quotations from the *Odyssey* of Homer are from the translation by E. V. Rieu in the Penguin Classics Series (1946).

> a mysterious human voice sang on in the dark; the voice of a boy or a woman, tremulous and sobbing, rose to an unbelievable pitch, was suddenly cut off, and sank so low it became as dark as the shadows, clinging to the fragrance of the frangipani, looping into arabesques and suddenly dropping with all its crystalline weight

which remained crucial in a spiritual diaspora that took him to Rangoon, Ceylon, Batavia, and Singapore from 1927 to 1932. At one extreme it compelled an erotic and solitary confrontation with the ineffable—an encounter which was thereafter constantly to force the poet "to find this music so that I might listen to it" at moments of incongruous political engagement, and invite the special angularity and privacy of his Odes, his *Book of Vagaries* and his *Skystones.*

At the other extreme, Neruda explains, it was precisely in the epoch of his *Residences*—a limbo of maximum sensuality and maximum intro-spection when he had "never read with so much pleasure or so volumi-nously"—Joyce, Lawrence, Rilke, Blake, Leonard and Virginia Woolf, "kilometers of English novels," the *poètes maudits*—that he found himself "returning to Rimbaud, Quevedo, or Proust" to track the enigma of his "voices" to an unexpectedly rational conclusion.

> *Swann's Way* made me experience all over again the torments, the loves and jealousies of my adolescence. And I realized that in the phrase from Vinteuil's sonata, a musical phrase Proust referred to as "aerial and fragrant," one savors not only the most exquisite description of sensuous sound, but also a desperate measure of passion itself.

With the aid of musicologists and musicians he pursued the phrase from Vinteuil through Schubert, Wagner, Saint-Saëns, Fauré, and d'Indy, to its source in César Franck's "Sonata for Piano and Violin" where, Neruda was convinced, there was finally "no room for doubt. Vinteuil's phrase was *there* . . .", "losing itself in the depths of the shadows, falling in pitch, prolonging, enhancing its agony . . . building in anguish like a Gothic structure, volutes repeated on and on, swayed by the rhythm that lifts a slender spire endlessly upward."

Very fittingly, the theme which concludes his chapter on "Luminous Solitude" is the same that led Odysseus to the islands where the Sirens "who bewitch everybody that approaches them" cast their spell on the unwary mariner "as they sit there in a meadow piled high with the mouldering skeletons of men": the theme of unearthly devastation, primordial melancholy, sonal enigma—the poetics of the inscrutable, which is the pervasive signature of his *Residencia en la tierra* (*Residence on Earth*). "No seaman," sing Homer's fatal sisters, "ever sailed his black ship past this spot without listening to the sweet tones that flow from our lips, and none that listened has not been delighted and gone on a wiser man." Similarly Neruda observes

> In his sharp-sighted narrative about a dying society he loved and hated, Proust, the greatest exponent of poetic realism, lingered with passionate indulgence over many works of art, paintings and cathedrals, actresses, books. But although his insight illuminated whatever it touched, he often went back to the enchantment of this sonata and its renascent phrase with an intensity that he probably did not give to any other descriptive passages. His words led me to relive my own life, to recover the hidden sentiments I had almost lost within myself in my long absence. I wanted to see in that musical phrase of Proust's magical narrative and I was swept away on music's wings . . . Savage darkness came down like a fist on my house among the coconut trees of Wella-watte, but each night the sonata lived with me, leading me on, welling around me, filling me with its everlasting sadness, its victorious melancholy.

The justice of this extraordinary gloss on the "bitter style" of the *Residences* that "worked systematically toward my own destruction" can hardly be overestimated. It is one of the major *données* of the *Memoirs* that students of the "lives" and the oeuvre of Neruda will have to reckon with in evoking the amplitude of his vision. For the whole Proustian-Homeric mix of "poetic realism and a dying society" with the meanderings of that most lachrymose and accident-prone of exemplary exiles, Odysseus of Ithaca, is *there*: wars, usurpations, betrayals, geographical and sexual peril, "the woes and the furies," the Sirens, the mysteries. Elsewhere in his *Memoirs* Neruda pauses for another of his typical reversals of context, in the service of a dialectical counter-myth. Of his first book he says, in italics: "I have always maintained that the writer's task has nothing to do with mystery or magic, and that the poet's, at least, must be a personal effort for the benefit of all. The closest thing to poetry is a loaf of bread or a ceramic dish or a piece of wood lovingly carved, even if by clumsy hands." Polemicists have already elevated this rubric of the *lares* and *penates* to extravagant heights of the sacrosanct; but Neruda's mandate to his interpreters is clear.

For all his repudiation of the Far East as an "influence on the poems" of *Residencia en la tierra* ("I say that this business of influence is mistaken."), it is the Siren-song of the mysteries—the phrase from Vinteuil or César Franck or the androgynous singers in Colombo—which in India and Malaysia were never far from the human misery of things—that stayed with Neruda to the end. "The esoteric philosophy of the Oriental countries," one may readily concede, can be dismissed as a "by-product of anxiety, neurosis, confusion, and opportunism of the West," or a "crisis in the guiding principles of capitalism." The music of enigma, however, exactly placed in Homer, as in Proust and Neruda, as a tutelary episode to convey his hero through the epical threshold that led him, with the aid of some stout twine and exemplary seamanship, to the restorations of Ithaca, cannot be overlooked.

It is the *music* that one hears, in any number of keys and baffling registers, all explicitly professed, in the later work of Pablo Neruda: in *Odes*, in the chants of his *Cantos ceremoniales*, the sea chanteys of his *La Barcarola*, the "sonatas" of his *Memorial de Isla Negra*, the "chansons de geste" of his *Canciones de gesta*, his *100 Love Sonnets*, or little love songs "hewn out of wood," and finally, his posthumous *Elegía*. This *scoring* and rescoring of whole volumes to engage sonal intangibles of the ordinary is never absent from the oeuvre of Pablo Neruda; nor is its function a purely cosmetic or programmatic one. Its effect is to alter the pitch and intensity of a vision, skew all the wavelengths to higher frequencies of the irrational, and invite all the permutations of oddity, vagary, and "extravagance" of his "late" style. Its intonation, wayward or droll at some times, delphic and incantatory at others, psychologically dense or colloquial at others, pays homage to the abiding priorities of mystery, bewitches by bafflement and surprise, and denies the reader the linear consolations of historicity.

More subtly and equivocally, it leads to that special provenance of islands and oceans that mingles process with enigma, materiality with the inscrutable, evanescence with the unalterable, which one associates with both Homer and Neruda. No reader of the lives of Pablo Neruda can miss the singing of his Sirens. It clings to the seascapes, the citadels, and the geological fantasies of Isla Negra, dominates his watery perspectives, and constitutes the very axis on which the evocations of the *Memoirs* are made to revolve in the Eternal Present. His insular and oceanic gods work themselves into the very fabric and time of his story as persistently as Poseidon and Athene weave their theophanies into the fortunes of Odysseus:

> Immersed in these memories [Neruda writes, as if to a Muse], I suddenly have to wake up. It's the sound of the sea. I am writing in Isla Negra, on the coast near Valparaiso. The ocean—rather than my watching it from my window, it watches me with a thousand eyes of foam . . . Years that are so far away! Reconstructing them, it's as if the sound of the waves I hear now touched something inside me again and again . . . I shall take up those images without attention to chronological order, just like these waves that come and go.

And midway in his concluding chapter, pathetically fragmented by the ravages of cancer and the perfidies of his "Cruel, Beloved Homeland," he notes:

> Solitude and multitude will go on being the primary obligations of the poet in our time. In solitude, the battle of the surf on the Chilean coast made my life richer. I was intrigued by and have loved passionately the battling waters and the rocks they battled against, the teeming ocean life, the impeccable formations of the "wandering bird," the splendor of the sea's foam.

IV

Compared with Eros, the provenance of Mars does not seem to require the labors of an exegete to make its pertinence felt. It has been thrust on the total accomplishment of Neruda by partisans of all political faiths over the years, bearing down from every direction; and in South America it still passes for the operative context of a simple-minded poetics of "the poet in the streets." To think of Neruda is to think of wars, revolutions, slogans, presidiums, dictators, falanges, duces; to be Marxist, Communist, Popular Unitarian, consul, senator, ambassador, presidential incumbent; to walk with Stalin, Nehru, Ho Chi Minh, Allende, and Frei. Despite all his later disclaimers, Neruda materializes for his countrymen again and again, cap-a-pie, on the battlements of Europe as in his native Chile, rattling sabers and dispensing a poetry of the barricades that would put Homer to global shame. For South American and Soviet readers, he remains the poet of an *Iliad* rather than an *Odyssey*; and his *Memoirs* make it clear that he is in part accountable for these confusions.

Almost too neatly, the odyssey turns into an iliad on the final page of his chapter on "Luminous Solitude": "And this Hitler, whose name appears from time to time in the newspapers," Neruda asks the Jewish consul of Batavia:

> "—this anti-Semite, anti-Communist leader, don't you think he can assume power?"
> "Impossible," he told me.
> "Why impossible, when history is full of the most absurd incidents?"
> "But you don't know Germany," he stated flatly. "That's the one place where it is absolutely impossible for a mad agitator like him to run even a village."

The chapters that follow drum up a veritable fanfare of militant subtitles. Their rhetoric is martial, their pace stertorous, their rapid dispersals and regroupings in "another part of the field," melodramatic: Chapter V: "Spain in My Heart," Chapter VI: "I Went Out to Look for the Fallen," Chapter VII: "Mexico, Blossoming and Thorny," Chapter VIII: "My Country in Darkness," Chapter IX: "Beginning and End of Exile," and so on, to Chapter X, recounting his "Voyage and Homecoming" like a nephew of Odysseus or Agamemnon. All is seen in either the stopped motion of hallucinatory close-ups of García Lorca, Arellano Marin ("a diabolical character,") Napoleon Ubico, González Videla ("a Chilean Judas," an "amateur tyrant on the saurian scale," "an acrobat who played to all sides,") Ilya Ehrenburg, Miguel Asturias, Jules Supervielle, Nehru, Mao Tze Tung, etc., etc.—or in frantically accelerated time-lapse, where one catches glimpses of the hero between flickery and snowy sub-titles: "A Congress in Madrid," "The Masks and the War," "Nazis in Chile," "Anthology of Pistols," "Macchu Pichu," "The Nitrate Pampa," "A Road in the Jungle," "The Andean Mountains," "In Paris with a Passport," "In the Soviet Union," "India Revisited," "My First Visit to China," "Wine and War," "Palaces Retaken," "Era of the Cosmonauts."

Here the cross-cutting becomes almost too clipped for comfort. Neruda's nightmarish flight over the Andes, for example, is picaresque rather than "Homeric": there is more freight than the *Memoirs* or the enforced escalation of its recovery can bear. Nevertheless the epical intonation remains. Episodes and identities fade in and wipe out like swamp gas, replete with villains, braggarts, demi-gods, princes, champions and the place-gods who preside over battlefields and destinies. Elsewhere, the heroes sulk in their tents: Pandit Jawaharlal Nehru (a "man with a bilious

complexion" who "must be going through a bad physical, political or
emotional experience,") Mao Tze Tung ("I saw hundreds of persons
waving a little red book, the universal panacea for winning at ping-pong,
curing appendicitis, and solving political problems."), Stalin ("Stalin
cultivated his mysteriousness systematically," he was "a man who was his
own prisoner.") while the battle broadens, or idles, or sweeps to a fratri-
cidal climax. Most conspicuous and passionate of all are the two minor
holocausts which recapitulate each other with eerie identity of detail: the
Spanish Civil War, in which Neruda's "House of Flowers" in Madrid
"caught between two fronts," was eventually "smashed to smithereens"
by Falangist artillery, with shrapnel "on the floor among my books"; and
the civil war in his native Chile, in whose aftermath, we are informed by a
Chronology, "his house in Valparaiso and the one in Santiago, where his
wake was held, had been ransacked and vandalized."

Curiously enough, the global paroxysms of Kapital, like World War
II, register as little more than a premonitory murmur: according to
Neruda, he was in possession of information, while still Consul General of
Chile in Mexico, which led him to anticipate Japan's entry into the War
one week before the bombing of Pearl Harbor. The ghastly duration of
that war, however, seems as remote to Neruda as Achilles' or Hektor's
awareness of the wars of Rameses II and the rise of Tiglath-Pileser in the
time of Ilium and Achaea. For Neruda, the operative front, apparently,
was elsewhere: in the New Russia or the New China, or those mini-nations
of Spain and South America where the readings on the Richter scale were
still only symptomatic, or hispanic, or provincial. Behind, and to one side
of the Iron Curtain, Neruda's busy-ness was incessant: red carpet deputa-
tions of inquiry or adulation in which Eluard or Aragon or Alberti was
elevated, Allende and Castro canonized, Stalin apotheosized and then extenuated, Nehru and Chairman Mao regarded with a fishy eye, and
González Videla and Francisco Franco consigned to the nethermost circle
of obloquy in polar blocks of rhetoric.

A second front, often as deadly and intimate as the permutations of
Eros, was the professional front on which Neruda's genius was drawing to
itself the lethal fire of the envious: persecutions from within and without
by *criticones*, poetasters, trend-setters, vandalous international factions: a
punishing ordeal of implacable and venal detraction. Here also Neruda
intervenes to consign his old malefactors to their appropriate circles of

damnation and posthumous ignominy. On the other hand, there are sinecures and orders of merit, almost equally political, which Neruda confers upon talents of good will: Paul Eluard, called "The Magnificent," the ubiquitous Ilya Ehrenberg, Quasimodo, Italian translator of Neruda, Gabriela Mistral, Alberti, Picasso, Siqueiros, Rivera, Darío, and the novelists of the South American "boom." Whitman is mentioned rather minimally on four occasions, Baudelaire on six, Proust at great length and with conspicuous fervor, on two. Of Eliot, Neruda records that he had to lock himself into a bathroom to escape the bewitchment of his verses, much as his Homeric namesake lashed himself to a mast to neutralize the music of the Sirens, while Eliot went on reading through the door.

> Eliot used to read my poems . . . And I was flattered . . . No one understood them better . . . Then one day he started to read me his own, and I ran off, selfishly, protesting: "Don't read them to me, don't read them to me . . ." I was depressed . . . Eliot has so much talent . . . He can draw. He writes essays . . . But I want to keep (my) reader, to preserve him, to water him like an exotic plant.

On César Vallejo, tiresomely paired with Neruda as continental contenders for the Hispanic Fleece, Neruda is characteristically astute and acerb. He addresses himself to the whole protocol of vogue and exposes the tactics of Vallejistas both at home and abroad:

> Vallejo was serious and pure in heart . . . I have written two poems, on different occasions, about my dear friend, my good comrade . . . In the last few years, during the small literary war kept alive by little soldiers with ferocious teeth, Vallejo, César Vallejo's ghost, César Vallejo's absence, César Vallejo's poetry, have been thrown into the fight against me and my poetry. This can happen anywhere. The idea is to wound those who have worked hard, to say, "This is no good; but Vallejo was good." If Neruda were dead, they would throw him in against Vallejo alive.

V

Finally there is the equivocal domain of Themis—that Themis who, according to Telemachus, "looseth and gathereth the meetings of men," and in Homer, serves the double function of convening assemblies and presiding over feasts. How has the goddess of assemblies apportioned

Neruda his desserts, and where does her weight fall in the *Memoirs*? Anthropologists like Jane Harrison and Gilbert Murray have been hard put to penetrate the mysteries and prerogatives of her office; but all are agreed that her enclave is societal, oracular, normative. Themis is at once a keeper of the destinies and proprieties. According to Miss Harrison, she is "prophecy incarnate," the summoner to the agora and the sacramental banquet, "the stuff of which religions are made," the "herd instinct, custom, convention slowly crystallized into Law," the keeper of the mysteries to which man "owes obedience, to which he pays reverence," the "social imperative," the guardian of the *polis* and the collective consciousness of men. Miss Harrison goes on to explain that "The Greek word, *Themis*, and the English word, *Doom* are, philology tells us, one and the same . . . Out of many *themistes* arose Themis. These *themistes* stood to the Greek for all he held civilized. They were the bases alike of his kingship and of his democracy . . . the ordinances of what must be done, what society compels . . . They are also the prophecies of what shall be in the future: they are also the dues, the rites, the prerogatives of a king, whatever custom assigns to him or any official."

One is tempted to translate the word straightway into the philosophical and political vulgate: for "Themis," read "categorical imperative," or "dialectical materialism," or Hegelian due process of History. However, the "phrase from Vinteuil" demands a magical rather than a Marxist rendering. In the spirit of "Homeric" mystery, Neruda's operative word for it in the Complete Words was *"deberes,"* or "responsibilities." Its persistence in the total canon of Neruda as the bard's mandate to render unto Moscow the things that are Moscow's, and unto Art the things which are Art's, is resolute, low-keyed, and non-negotiable. It is Neruda's way of serving notice that he will write a partisan pastiche like *Las uvas y el viento* (*The Grapes and the Wind*: 1954) or an *Incitación al Nixonicidio y alabanza de la revolución chilena* (*Incitation to Nixonicide and Praise for the Chilean Revolution*: 1973) whenever the occasion calls for one, and an *Estravagario* (*Book of Vagaries*: 1958) or a *Piedras del cielo* (*Skystones*: 1970) whenever the vagaries and solitude of things move him to listen to his Sirens.

Similarly, his *deberes* to Themis in the prose Life are reaffirmed in a massive penultimate chapter called "Poetry Is An Occupation." The Spanish here rendered as "occupation," *"oficio,"* is pure Jane Harrison, and embraces such private and sacerdotal "occupations" as "The Power of Poetry," "Living with the Language," "Critics Must Suffer," "Short and

Long Lines," "Originality," "Literary Enemies," "Criticism and Self-Criticism," and finally, when all the stables have been swept and justice administered to friend and enemy alike, a glimpse at Elysium itself, "The Nobel Prize." Reflecting on "Short and Long Lines" he writes:

> I started life more naked than Adam, but with my mind made up to maintain the integrity of poetry . . . Poetry with a capital P, was shown respect. Not only poetry, but poets as well. . . . The poet who is not a realist is dead. And the poet who is only a realist is also dead. The poet who is only irrational will only be understood by himself and his beloved, and this is very sad. The poet who is all reason will be understood even by jackasses, and this is also terribly sad.

And he concludes the section as a whole with a resounding invocation to the *polis* of the "social imperative" of poets:

> Poetry is a deep inner calling in man; from it came liturgy, the psalms, and also the content of religions. The poet confronted nature's phenomena and in early ages called himself a priest. In the same way, to defend his poetry, the poet of the modern age accepts the investiture earned in the street, among the masses. Today's social poet is still a member of the earliest order of priests.

It is precisely here that the significance of these stocktakings needs to be anchored as a culminating "permutation of Themis." The pattern that emerges from the whole of the *Memoirs* is ritual, conservative, reverential, rather than "revolutionary"—a comely and civilized insistence on the decorum of the poet's obligations to his state, to his self, and to biological process. For all his "bohemian" penchant for "eccentrics," it is the decorum of the constitutional way and the old sacrament of marriage—a kind of ethos of spiritual seemliness—that Neruda came to affirm, just as Homer divinized the legitimacy of his hero's functions as exemplary husband, house-cleaner, and Prince of Ithaca. Even in the conduct of his favorite revolutions Neruda everywhere implies the constitutional and responsible way: polls, plebecites, and peace, rather than assassinations. Nothing was more abhorrent to Neruda, it is clear, than the mindless subversion of consent by hooligans, cynics, and conspiratorial anarchists —the cartoon of a Beard with a Bomb in its pocket:

> When the reactionary right had to depend on terrorism, [he writes] it used it unscrupulously . . . General Schneider, the army chief of staff, a

respected and respectable man who opposed a *coup d'état* to prevent
Allende's succession to the Presidency of the republic, was assassinated
. . . The gang was made up of young members of the social set and professional delinquents . . . Blocked everywhere by diabolical and legal
obstacles, the Chilean road was at all times strictly constitutional.

Elsewhere he writes of "Extremism and Spies":

Former anarchists—and the same will happen tomorrow to the anarchists of today—very often drift off toward a very comfortable position,
anarcho-capitalism, the refuge of political snipers, would-be leftists,
and false liberals. All those individualist rebels are delighted, one way
or the other, by the reactionary know-how, the strong-arm method that
treats them as heroic defenders of sacrosanct principles . . . I saw all this
in Spain during the war.

Of guerilla tactics in the abstract, he notes:

Guerilla methods in Latin America opened the floodgates to all sorts of
squealers. The spontaneous character and the youth of these organiza-
tions made it hard to detect and unmask spies . . . this cult of risk was
encouraged by the romantic spirit and the wild Guerilla theories that
swept Latin America . . . For a long time the supporters of this tactic
saturated the continent with theses and documents that virtually allot-
ted the popular revolutionary government of the future, not to the
classes exploited by capitalism, but to all and sundry armed groups.
The flaw in this line of reasoning is its political weakness: it is sometimes possible for a great guerilla and a powerful political mind to
coexist, as in the case of Che Guevara, but that is an exception and
wholly dependent on chance.

And of the Achilles' heel of Soviet protocol, he concedes:

The existence of Soviet dogmatism in the arts for long periods of time
cannot be denied, but it should also be mentioned that this dogmatism
was always considered a defect and combatted openly . . . Life is stronger and more obstinate than precepts. The revolution is life; precepts
prepare their own grave.

It is in this sense that the true title of his *Memoirs* comes full circle,
insists on itself, and achieves its full force as a confessional affirmation of
the Virtue of all Action. "I have *lived*!" is the *"oficio"* of the activist. For

Neruda, as for Blake, the rites of the *polis*—whether it be Santiago, Stalingrad, or England's "green and pleasant land,"—and the hierophantic service of Themis, were no fossilized barrow of bones. On the contrary, they comprised an autonomous *life*—life Homerically conceived as a movement from herd instinct to Law, a convening of feasts and assemblies, a commitment to the mysteries and the prerogatives of a "social imperative," a ceremonious embodiment of fidelity. The simplicity and comeliness of Neruda's life-long *deberes* as a card-carrying summoner to the congresses and calling of his party is finally as obvious as the piety of Odysseus. The tone of his chapter on *"oficios"* is millenial, messianic, pacific, as in the 24th Book of the *Odyssey*, when

> Athene called out at once to Odysseus, by his
> royal titles, commanding him to hold his hand
> and bring this civil strife to a finish, for fear
> of offending the ever-watchful Zeus.
> Odysseus obeyed her, with a happy heart.

Similarly Neruda writes in a late poem of "Summation":

> I am glad of the great obligations (*deberes*)
> I imposed on myself. In my life
> many strange and material things have crowded together—
> fragile wraiths that entangled me,
> categorical, mineral hands,
> an irrational wind that dismayed me,
> barbed kisses that scarred me, the hard reality
> of my brothers,
> my implacable vow to keep watchful,
> my penchant for loneliness—to keep to myself
> in the frailty of my personal whims.
> This is why—water on stone—my whole life has
> sung itself out between chance and austerity.

In the same chapter Neruda, after "the death of the Cyclops of the Kremlin" (meaning Stalin), when the "human jungle shuddered," quotes from a page of Ilya Ehrenburg: "Pablo is one of the few happy men I have known." He goes on to invoke the delights of Themis in an uncluttered assertion that "We poets have the right to be happy, as long as we are close to the people of our country and in the thick of the fight for their happiness . . . In my party, Chile's Communist Party, I found a large group of simple people who had left far behind them personal vanity, despotism, material interests. I felt happy knowing honest people who were fighting for common decency, for justice." It was, for Neruda, a happiness not unmixed with the mischief of loyal insubordination, as his preference for his *Book of Vagaries*, above all its competitors in the canon of his *Obras*, makes clear:

> Of all my books, *Estravagario* is not the one that sings the most, but the one that has the best leaps. Its leaping poems skip over distinction, respect, mutual protection, establishments, and obligations (*las obligaciones*) to sponsor reverent irreverence. Because of its disrespect, it's my most personal book. Because of its range, it is one of the most important. For my own taste, it's a terrific book, with the tang that the truth always has.

In more reverential guise, the last word in any Homeric reading of the works of Pablo Neruda must be reserved for the poet himself, who, in a sonnet to his Greek namesake, reaffirmed the mysteries and sanctities of Themis in a concluding sestet:

> Whoever sees you and never guesses all
> that was given you to know, will never know
> the magic of your tranquillity in motion.
>
> Compared to you, all arrogance is paltry,
> the rich, impoverished, and your constant honor, this:
> always to be secret and sonorous as the wind is.
>
> *(To Homer)*

12

Pablo Neruda:
Splendor and Death

Two themes recur during the twelve years of my correspondence with Pablo Neruda which register with devastating poignancy at this time: one personal, the other political and peripatetic. The first concerns a series of projected visits to the island which the last decade of his poetry has made legendary, and which fatality and contingency have now removed entirely from the realm of human procrastination: Isla Negra. Early in 1964—the year of Neruda's 60th birthday—he wrote to propose:

> Next June the University of Chile plans to celebrate my birthday. Unfortunately, there is no money for traveling expenses, but you can stay either with me or with friends in the event that you can afford the trip and decide to come to Chile. Many poets from a number of countries will be on hand, but your visit would be the best birthday present of all.

Three months later another letter followed, this time in an English scribble:

> Great news: the University of Chile invites you for the 12 of July paying the trip and return and one week hotel. You may stay with us as long as you like, there are no problems. Bureaucracy is here endless, yesterday the Faculty of Letters had to approve then to pass to the Council and so on, but the Rector told me yesterday that everything was approved, only the official notification etc. So you, I hope, will be with us and we will be so happy to receive the poet and the friend.

Shortly thereafter a third letter followed:

> At the last moment, the University found it had no funds to meet the cost of the round trip to Chile. Three invitations had been extended at my request: one to Artur Lundkvist of Sweden, one to Salvatore Quasimodo of Italy, and one to Ben Belitt of the United States. The Rector had already written the letters of invitation, reserved the passages, etc. Precisely at that moment the workers and employees of the University struck for higher wages. The employees won and we lost. I lost the most, dear Ben, since I had counted on many long talks with you and our getting better acquainted.

From that time on, invitation alternated with postponement, as circumstance, illness, or the time-table of our changing commitments continued to work against us over the years.

In 1966 Neruda wrote:

> I'm delighted to hear of your possible visit to Chile. Don't worry about expenses here. You'll live in my house in Isla Negra, we'll eat fried fish together, and you'll have time to work on your own, since there is plenty of space and affection to go round.

In October of 1967 there was another invitation to "come and live with us —months, weeks, days, or minutes—here in Isla Negra. It's Spring here now"; and I was forced to postpone my visit again. The following January there was further word:

> I was about to leave for Uruguay, but if you decide to come to Chile, I'll be delighted to stay on and wait for you, since I want you to spend some time with us here.

The letter was apparently mislaid by his secretary, Homero Arce, who wrote three days later to paraphrase its contents; and by an inadvertence well known to Americans at large in Mexico, my answer seems never to have reached Isla Negra at all. On March 31, 1968, there was a further note:

> Dear Ben, salud! Isla Negra awaits you, we are counting on a visit in January, 1970. Why not spend New Years Eve with us?

And on February 9, 1971:

I would have loved for you to visit us this summer. Now that's impossible, since in a very few days we will be leaving for Paris, where I
have been designated Ambassador.

Then, only three weeks before the usurpation of Chile by the military
Junta, when all was in readiness—passport, sabbatical, a Bennington
travel grant, and an ideal coincidence of circumstances—I had the last
letter I was to receive from Neruda:

I've undergone so many changes of secretary that I hardly know if I
answered your last letter in time, suggesting a visit to come. I'm
tempted to say: better wait till my 70th birthday next July, but perhaps
you could make that the occasion of another visit. Another good date
would be the coming New Year's Eve. If none of these dates is feasible,
come whenever you please, since our house is always open to you.

I shall never eat fried fish with Neruda at Isla Negra: never interview,
query, badger, or consult with him in the forensic vein which journalists
over the world have turned into such picturesque and controversial copy. I
shall never have been wholly alone with him. He remains enigmatic,
inaccessible, solitary, unencountered. My few contacts with him yield
only public images. I remember the sophisticated self-effacement of his
posture at a luncheon given by Archibald MacLeish at the Century Club
in the first days of his visit to this country in June, 1968; how his fantasy
fixed on a bottle-green wall in an upper story of the Grove Press warren of
public and private environments, while the guests circled like attacking
Indians, drinking, in many languages, and rooting among the hors-
d'oeuvres—how he *fastened* on the wall, as though he would add it to his
other curiosities at Isla Negra, and repeated in his heavylidded way:
"Now I would call that an *edible* green!" I remember his shrewdness, his
courtesy, his melancholy: the rigor with which he contained the homage
of hundreds jamming the walls of the Kaufman Auditorium, waiting to
be inflamed by a facile political innuendo; how he turned away, after one
idolatrous curtain call and an armful of roses, gestured to the evening's
triumphant entrepeneuse, and said: "Let's go out the back way." To my
surprise, a battery of Chilean *paparazzi* were waiting there with poised
cameras, just as the audience itself and his hotel lobby seemed laced with
a cadre of cultural and ambassadorial attachés. There, Neruda paused and

posed briefly, with an apologetic aside: "Excuse me, but this is something I have to do." Then we followed him into a cab and headed toward the Fifth Avenue Hotel. On his last visit of all, when he presided over a kind of intricate levée in a corner of the salon at the Center for Inter-American Relations and all was virtually immobilized by diplomatic protocol, came the last of his invitations—this time to *paella* at the Jai-Alai the following afternoon—which I was again compelled to "postpone."

The motif of travel is equally persistent and poignant—the endless displacements of a "sixty-year-old, smiling public man" pursuing his search for intimacy and the public *"deberes"* of a lifetime throughout the length and breadth of a country, a continent, a world. He seemed to encircle its geography like a line of latitude, always arriving from an extended tour of readings, as global custodian of Spanish letters, or departing in his character as circuit-rider for a political party and an abiding national vision. His very first letter, in March, 1961, apologizes for the delay occasioned by his recent "return to Chile after a year abroad." On March 7, 1963, he wrote again (in English) to say:

> I was seven months away, between the Caucasus and Milan, then I arrived and started in reading my poems from North to South of Chile, changing place once or twice a day for some two months. Now with a lumbago I am having thermical waters very high in the barren Cordillera and profit of my first peace moments . . . I am writing an autobiographical long poem to appear in July 1964. I will have 60 years then . . . My dear friend please excuse my wandering life.

On May 27, 1964, he wrote to explain:

> I went far away saying my poems to great (40,000) or small (500) public meetings, as it is in September the great event, the election of the President, and the country is full of calm electricity. As you know, perhaps, this is a very legalist nation and the votes are to be conquered one by one.

On May 24, 1966, shortly before his visit to the States, there was a note on sky-blue paper under his private heraldry of a fish in two intersecting circles of latitude and longitude—half in the green ink (which he may have borrowed from Gomez de la Serna), and half in red crayon (with the marginal explanation: "Ink finished!"):

As you see, dear Ben, it is a question of some days to meet. I'll arrive with Matilde on the sixth to the 5th Av. Hotel in that Avenue, and on the 11 will be the reading. What will be the choice? I am at a lost. Won't you illuminate me writing to N. York? And when shall we see you? I like that idea of going everywhere and California to read. Is it not too much?

Needless to say, a program of readings had already been worked out by the Poetry Center in an agonizing protocol of equity among the available translators. However, he did cross the country at the invitation of Luis Monguió of the University of California, with the mixed motive of reading his poetry and gathering Americana for his "bandit-play" about the Gold Rush in the sierras of Calaveras County, "Splendor and Death of Joaquín Murieta." On August 20, 1968, Neruda wrote in a more hilarious mood congratulating me on my "resurrection" from the dead, after rumors, mysterious and shocking to us both, about my recent demise:

> The important thing is that your feet are firmly on the ground and you are fully extant . . . I am about to leave for a trip—a new book (*Las manos del día*) and a new edition of my Complete Works is about to appear in Buenos Aires. Later I will be going to Rio de Janeiro where a new anthology of my poetry and a record of the *20 Poems* will appear. From there I leave for Caracas, then to Colombia and finally to Mexico. I have been invited to attend the Olympics(!) Perhaps I'll end up in Canada at the end of October. Can't we meet somewhere in this long itinerary?

When he wrote me in November of that month to say: "We are *not* travelling in 1969!" the announcement came at the top of the page, over the address and dateline, with the air of a miraculous dispensation. The very next message, however, a postcard from the volcano country of Ensenada, with an invitation to join him on his 65th birthday, concludes: "I am very tired. One month of hard travel." His next letter referred to a sojourn "in a lake island"; then came France: then the United States again; then Isla Negra and Santiago in 1972.

II

I do not know how to elegize Pablo Neruda or suggest the magnitude of his loss at a time when he himself was completing the Autobiographies

—begun ten years before under the working title of "Lives of a Poet"—
that were to celebrate his 70th birthday, just as the *"Memorial de Isla
Negra"* struck the medal for his 60th birthday. It is hardly sufficient to say
that for Neruda, living and dying constituted a continuum of mysterious
impurities which he affirmed with increasing gaiety of vision, even when
illness and violence threatened due process of mortality, in the end. He
could write of himself:

> Careful, they said: don't slip
> on the wax of the ballroom:
> look out for the ice and the rain and the mud.
> Right! we all answered: this winter
> we'll live without slippage!
> And what happened? Under our feet
> we felt something give way,
> and there we were, up to our hunkers
>
> in the blood of a century . . .
>
> Maybe others will live out their lives with
> no more than an occasional spill on the ice.
>
> I live with this horror: when I tumble,
> I go down in blood.
>
> ("El peligro")

or his century:

> What a litter death has strewn
> in the glens of our century!
> Surely the She-Goat who whores for us all
> at her games with the world,
> left us a planet in ruins
> crammed with the refuse of skeletons,
> prairies bombed off the map
> in a rubble of cities mangled
> and toothless with fire,
> cities charred and abandoned
> whose streets offer nothing
> but the quiet that burns in the holocaust.
>
> ("Otra vez")

or of a "sick man in the sun":

What would it profit you, now as good as dead, if Monday came
round again, ripe as a kiss, woven with sun,
loosened its place in the sky
and aimed its full force at your worsening crisis?

. . . Yes, should you die on such a day,
not only would nothing have happened,
but no festival would ever have equalled
the measure of this one, the heyday of your burial.

("El enfermo toma el sol")

The death of Neruda in the fullness of his powers and the heyday of
his confidence in the integrity of Chile as "a very legalist nation" where
"the votes are to be conquered one by one" is not a festival, but a mas-
sacre. Only now, the probity of his commitment to a democratic way,
whatever his politics, can be seen in the midst of all that remains sinister
and dubious: the heroism of his old repudiations of a Chile where process
was aborted by violence from within and without, the purgatorial mili-
tance of his exile in the bad days of González Videla, the extraordinary
purity of his allegiances and *"deberes"* (debts) in a continent wracked by
power vacuums and political recidivism. From the perspective of his death
and the grim encapsulation of Chile in another bloody vacuum, it is clear
that *process was all* in Neruda's vision of the redemptive impurity of things
—that liberty was inseparable from the pursuit of *ends* in terms of genu-
inely liberating *means*: what Blake called the "spiritual gifts" of a committed man "saying his poems" to great audiences and small in behalf of a
"great event, the election of a President," from which our mountebanks of
Watergate and the Central Intelligence Agency have much to learn.

It is this circumstance that makes his absence seem so suddenly explosive, like the removal of a king-pin from the incomprehensible shambles
of South American polity—the falling-apart of a continent's last venture
in fidelity, unloosing "mere anarchy" upon a world where before, a poet
came and went in an atmosphere "full of calm electricity," conquering
votes, one after another, until the cabinet of Allende legitimately succeed-
ed to the cabinet of Frei.

For readers still obsessed with the priorities of the *Residencias*, the
Odes, and "Macchu Picchu," missing

the perpetual motion of
a man both confused and committed,
a man at once joyful, torrential,
energetic, and autumnally prodigal

("Testamento de otoño")

his death should also give new perspective to the achievement of the "later" Neruda: *Estravagario* (1958), *Cien sonetos de amor* (1960), *Plenos poderes* (1962), *Memorial de Isla Negra* (1964), his secular vision of the "last things" of a century, *Fin de mundo* (1969), his *Skystones*, and his curiously mistitled (and untranslated) *Geografía infructuosa* (1972), where instead of a "Barren Geography" we have both the full sound of "masked and immobilized time" and the new elegance of his residence in Paris. It is a splendor not to be misprized or misunderstood. The total oeuvre of Pablo Neruda, which before seemed a deafening horseshoe of rainbows supporting the downpour of Genesis itself or a system of planets and suns like Andromeda, can now be viewed as a continuum as well as a quantum. In the title poem of his "Full Powers," Neruda observed characteristically:

I never tire of coming and going,
death never closes my way with a stone,
I never weary of being and non-being . . .

All I know is: I keep moving, I move to be moving.
I sing because I sing because I sing.

Surely it is time to replace the old, square cartography of causes and effects which have polarized his admirers, with a new system of soundings, a stranger table of elements. Cues are everywhere present in the total amalgam of his "comings and goings": in his shift from private and public causes, to enigmas; from songs of myself, general songs, and elemental odes, to universals; from last wills and testaments, to last judgments; from "the stones of Chile," to "the stones of the sky," from impurities to transparencies; from history to mystery:

So it goes: I was shaped out of nullity
like the sea battering away at a reef,
with briny capsules of whiteness,
pulling the pebbles back with the waves . . .
However death works to circle me in,
something opens a window to life in me.

("Plenos poderes")

The terminal "insularity" of the later Neruda is really another spiritual economy: on the one hand it raises his search for "process" to its highest power of subjective intensity. On the other, it takes us downward, through the flinty and igneous life, and outward, into the oceanic and aerial life, to prove that " no man is an island." The liquefaction of his vision into a "mighty arcana of water" that "shakes itself free" from "our transactions, the mines, motors, flags of our species" and "cleanses and cleanses"; and conversely, the mineralization of all, in three "books of stones," to "surpass what I cannot / search out, survive, partake / of the sleeper's metallic condition / and his burning beginnings," are functional as well as awesome. They constitute an answer, if enigmas are answerable, to the questions proposed at the very center of his political and geological song in *Canto General*: what nurtures the crab, the narwhal, the kingfisher, and the harpoonist?

> I answer you: Ocean will say it—the arc of its lifetime
> is vast as the seasand, flawless and numberless.
> Between cluster and cluster, the blood and the vintage
>   time brightens
> the flint in the petal, the beam in the jellyfish.

("Los enigmas")

These are the roots invoked by Neruda in the climactic outcry of his later vision of past things and last things in *"Fin de fiesta"* (1961): "What can I do without roots?" These preoccupations put depth under the purely topical, pathos under the quotidian, metaphysics under the "brutal imperative" that "makes warriors of us . . . gives us the stance / and inflection of fighters." These help us to measure Neruda's rigors as warrior and fighter, and encompass the assimilative bounties of his harvest as gardener of a continent, cultivating the garden of his "barren geography," making the wasteland fruitful.

BEN BELITT:
A SELECTIVE BIBLIOGRAPHY
OF TRANSLATIONS

BOOKS

Four Poems by Rimbaud: The Problem of Translation. Denver, Swallow, 1947; London, Sylvan Press, 1948, Theodore Brun Ltd., 1949.

Poet in New York: Federico García Lorca. New York, Grove Press, 1955; London, Thames and Hudson, 1956. Editor and Translator.

Selected Poems of Pablo Neruda. New York, Grove Press, 1961. Editor and Translator.

Juan de Mairena: Epigrams, Maxims, Memoranda, and Memoirs of an Apocryphal Professor with An Appendix of poems from *The Apocryphal Songbooks*, by Antonio Machado. Berkeley, University of California Press, 1963. Editor and Translator.

Selected Poems of Rafael Alberti. Berkeley, University of California Press, 1966. Editor and Translator.

A New Decade: Poems 1958-67, by Pablo Neruda. New York, Grove Press, 1969. Editor and Translator.

Splendor and Death of Joaquín Murieta (drama) by Pablo Neruda. New York, Farrar, Straus and Giroux, 1972. Editor and Translator. London, Alcove Press, 1973.

New Poems, 1968-1970, by Pablo Neruda. New York, Grove Press, 1973. Editor and Translator.

Five Decades: Poems 1925-1970, by Pablo Neruda. New York, Grove Press, 1974. Editor and Translator.

MISCELLANEOUS

Poems from The Canto General, by Pablo Neruda. New York, Racolin Press, 1968. With 10 original lithographs, 23" by 41", by David Alfaro Siqueiros. Edition of 235 copies numbered and signed by artist, typeface "Romaine du Roi," from presses of Fernand Mourlot, Paris.

To Painting / A la pintura, by Rafael Alberti. West Islip, New York, Universal Art Editions, 1972. With original aquatints by Robert Motherwell. 24

unbound pages, 25½" by 38". Edition of 50 copies, signed by artist, Tatyana
Grosman, Director.

The Selected Poems of García Lorca. New York, New Directions, 1955. Translator,
with others.

Cántico: Selections, by Jorge Guillén, Boston, Little Brown, 1965. Translator with
others.

Selected Poems, by Eugenio Montale, New York New Directions 1965. Translator,
with others.

Selected Poems 1923-1967, by Jorge Luis Borges. New York, Delacorte Press,
1972. Translator, with others.

Eight Poems, by Vicente Aleixandre, in *Mundus Artium*, University of Ohio,
Athens, Ohio, pp. 8-35, Vol. II, No. 3, 1969.

Fourteen Lyrics, by Federico García Lorca, in *Quarterly Review of Literature*, Princeton University, Princeton, New Jersey, pp. 5-18, Vol. VI, No 1, 1950.

Fourteen Poems, by Enrique Huaco, in *Canto*, University of Massachusetts, An-
dover, Massachusetts, pp. 129-144, Vol. I, No. 2, 1977.

A Pinecone, a Toy Sheep . . . , by Pablo Neruda, (autobiography), in *The Evergreen
Review Reader* 1957-1967, New York, Grove Press, pp. 438-443, 1968.

The Switchman, by Juan José Arreola (short story), in *TriQuarterly*, Northwestern
University, Evanston, Illinois, pp. 185-192, Vol. 13/14, 1968-1969.

Lives of a Poet: In the Far East by Pablo Neruda (autobiography), in *Salmagundi*,
Skidmore College, Saratoga Springs, New York, pp. 3-17, Spring, 1972.

The Bourgeois King: A Droll Story, by Ruben Darío (short story), in *The Eye of the
Heart: Short Stories from Latin America*, Indianapolis/New York, Bobbs-
Merrill, pp. 44-48. 1973.

Introduction: The Achievement of Pablo Neruda by Luis Monguió (essay) in *Selected
Poems of Pablo Neruda*, New York, Grove Press, 1961, pp. 7-29.

Foreword: Antonio Machado as Poet and Philosopher by Segundo Serrano Poncela
(essay) in *Juan de Mairena*, Berkeley, University of California Press, 1963, pp.
vii-xxi.

The Poetry of Rafael Alberti: An Introduction by Luis Monguió (essay) in *Selected
Poems of Rafael Alberti*, Berkeley, University of California Press, 1966, pp. 1-
34.